Trevor Hudson's friendship has been a gift. He is an exceptional communicator who unpacks complex concepts in a way that is simultaneously accessible, practical, experiential, and memorable. Trevor has spent a lifetime learning from a host of "veterans of the Spirit." And all the attributes of the author, and his remarkable journey, are beautifully on display in this magnum opus work on discernment. Take this journey with Trevor and find your special "message to deliver," "song to sing," "act of love to bestow" . . . and the special friendship with God that is yours to enjoy.

GARY W. MOON, MDiv, PhD, founding executive director of the Martin Institute and the Dallas Willard Center, director of Conversatio Divina at Westmont College, and author of *Apprenticeship with Jesus* and *Becoming Dallas Willard*

Trevor Hudson's *In Search of God's Will* serves as an extensive field guide for those of us who long to discern what we are to do with this one life God has given us. Hudson, in his inimitable wisdom, demonstrates that we need not be anxious in our efforts to figure out God's path for us and God's big dream for the world. When we know Jesus, we know God— and that God is completely loving toward us. Indeed, Hudson expertly leads us on a journey wherein we discover God has tenderly provided everything we need to know him and his will for our lives.

MARLENA GRAVES, author of *Bearing God*

T0266560

*How can I learn to discern God's will?* is a question all Christians ask. We want our lives to matter. We don't want to wander off the path God has for us to travel. We want to journey well and wisely through our lives. How important it is to have a gentle, experienced guide as we walk with God. Trevor Hudson is just such a person. He has pondered discerning the will of God for a long time. Trevor provides a wise, tested road map for God's pilgrims in *In Search of God's Will*. Highly recommend.

> **CHRISTOPHER A. HALL**, distinguished professor emeritus of theology at Eastern University and past president of Renovaré

Grounded in Scripture, real-life experiences, and examples, *In Search of God's Will* provides steps for the journey of maturing as a disciple of Christ. In his characteristic simple but compelling way, Trevor reminds us we each have a unique, God-given "song to sing," which is discovered through discernment in order to be aligned with God's dream for the world. That discovery is what every follower of Christ longs for. I recommend this book as a resource for individuals and small groups seeking growth into Christlikeness.

> **REV. N. PURITY MALINGA**, presiding bishop of the Methodist Church of Southern Africa

What a journey of discovery into the will of God! With insight, humility, and sincerity, Trevor Hudson helps us unveil the very heart of God. Throughout this beautiful book we are invited to draw close enough to God to discover the secrets and beauty of his will.

> **PROF. STEPHAN JOUBERT**, leader of the South African echurch

We live in a chaotic and noisy world with many strange voices from the mass media, social media, and other sources competing for our attention and loyalty and seeking to program us in their own image. Trevor's latest offering is a generous and apt gift with practical steps to empower us to develop the spiritual art of discernment—listening to God and making right decisions for a time such as this.

REV. DR. SIDWELL MOKGOTHU, bishop of the Limpopo Synod of the Methodist Church of Southern Africa

In a wonderfully lucid and practical way, Trevor Hudson helps us grapple with fundamental Christian questions: *How do I hear God? What is God's will? What is God asking from me?* Born from Trevor's own experience of living discerningly, this book opens the door for us to find God in ways we might not expect. Masterfully written, it is a must-read for anyone seeking to live discerningly . . . and in so doing, walk more closely with Jesus.

RUSSELL POLLITT, SJ, director of the Jesuit Institute South Africa

As a pastor, I often encounter questions about God's will. I am so thankful for a guide to conversations and discernment around this important question. Trevor's book is both practical and full of pastoral wisdom.

TOM SMITH, pastor at Fontainebleau Community Church

In this book, Trevor Hudson engages us in the awe-inspiriting vision of how each of us is called in a unique and unrepeatable way to play our part in God's big dream for the world. We are invited on a journey to discover God's hopes and dreams for us. Trevor distills a wealth of wisdom from our Christian spiritual tradition, making it practical and accessible for every Christian seriously seeking to discover God's will. He shares heartwarming stories from his own discernment story showing the ups and downs of his journey of discovery. Trevor also invites us to engage in the simple yet powerful discernment exercises offered in each chapter. As we use the book, we become better able to sense the movement of the Holy Spirit and discover God's unfolding invitation in our own lives. This book is the fruit of a lifetime of learning how to live discerningly. I highly recommend it.

**DR. ANNEMARIE PAULIN-CAMPBELL,** head of spirituality at the Jesuit Institute South Africa

*In*

# SEARCH

*of*

# GOD'S

# WILL

*Discerning a Life of
Faithfulness and Purpose*

# TREVOR HUDSON

A NavPress resource published in alliance
with Tyndale House Publishers

*For Debbie, my dearest companion and codiscerner, as we have sought to discover God's will in our life together.*

---

*For Jo and James and Mark and Marike, as each of you seeks to become the person God wants you to be.*

# Contents

# Foreword

When I first sat down to read *In Search of God's Will*, I found myself recalling a season long ago when I toured as the opening act for Christian singer-songwriter Rich Mullins. Something about Rich's music touched people in vulnerable places; it often helped them become aware of their deepest longings. After each concert, I loved sitting next to Rich at the autograph table, unabashedly eavesdropping on his conversations with his listeners. Often, those conversations turned serious and urgent.

On a few occasions, I heard someone ask Rich how to discern God's will. Each time, Rich offered some surprising counsel.

"I don't think finding God's plan for you has to be complicated," he'd say. "God's will is that you love him with all your heart and soul and mind, and also that you love your neighbor as yourself. Get busy with that, and then, if God wants you to do something unusual, he'll take care of it. Say, for example, he wants you to go to Egypt." Rich would pause for a moment before flashing his trademark grin. "If that's the case, he'll provide eleven jealous brothers, and they'll sell you into slavery."

I'm not sure whether this satisfied Rich's fans, but I suspect his advice has stayed with them the same way it has with me. When I find myself wrestling with life decisions, I think of Rich's Egypt Principle. It makes me laugh, and then it asks me to get down to the serious business of determining which of my options best allows me to love God and other people. Such an approach usually rules out certain possibilities while affirming (and even creating) several others.

Sometimes, once I've narrowed down my alternatives in light of the Great Commandment, the determinative "jealous brothers" do show up. A scholarship comes through at one school rather than another. A job offer is escalated or rescinded. Other times, however, I'm left standing at the junction of several seemingly reasonable pathways, miserable with uncertainty. *How should I discern my next step?*[1]

The book you hold in your hands offers invaluable responses to that very question. Yes, Trevor Hudson affirms, God's "general will" is quite evident in Scripture. But discovering God's "personal will" for our lives requires us to develop our capacity for discernment. It involves reflecting on what Trevor calls the "outer landscape" of our lives (from the big "jealous brothers" events to the smaller nuances of our everyday experiences). Critically, it also invites us to attend to our "inner landscape," where, Trevor argues, our thoughts, feelings, and emotions "can become wonderful signals that point us to the leading of God's Spirit in our lives."

Trevor tells us that this process of discernment helps us discover not only what we are called to *do* but also whom we are uniquely called to *be*. "Each one of us is called to live the truth of our unrepeatable uniqueness," Trevor writes. Gently, thoughtfully, and persuasively, Trevor makes the case that learning to become ourselves may be even more fundamentally important than figuring out what to do—and that the two quests are inextricably linked.

Perhaps you, like me, have read John the Baptist's cry—"He must increase, but I must decrease" (John 3:30, KJV)—and imagined your personality gradually receding into a generic Christlikeness. We forget, of course, that the prophet praying that prayer only became more completely his confrontational, unshaven, locust-eating self in Jesus' presence. I like to think he became *Johnny-er* and *Johnny-er* until his *entire being* was pointing to Jesus.

When I first met Trevor Hudson, I was struck (like so many others) by his gentleness, his thoughtfulness, his posture of listening, and his giftedness in accompanying others into a deeper awareness of God's personal love. In the years since, Trevor has only become *Trevor-er*, and this book is the fruit of his long obedience. As you read it, please don't miss the opportunity to engage with the discernment exercises sprinkled throughout the pages. If you do, you will discover that you are invited to use all the particularity of your unrepeatable heart, your unique soul, and your one-of-a-kind mind to love God and your neighbor in the way that *only you* can. For this, friend, is the "good, pleasing and perfect will" of God (Romans 12:2, NIV).

*Carolyn Arends*
recording artist, author, and
Renovaré director of education

# Preface

Thank you for picking up this book. This theme of discerning God's personal will has a special place in my heart, and I hope it resonates with your heart too. In this preface I want to do just three things: tell you how this book came to be, share my hopes for it, and suggest how to enrich your reading experience.

## How This Book Came to Be

Through the course of over forty years of working closely with people as a pastor, I have come across many who long to find God's will for their life. They say things like "I wish I knew what God wants me to do," "I really need God's guidance right now," and "I don't know which decision God wants me to make." Perhaps you've said similar things. Or maybe some of the following scenarios sound more familiar.

- You sometimes wonder how you can know when God is communicating with you.
- You would like to learn more about how you can discern God's personal calling in your life.

- You are interested in exploring the relationship between what God desires and your own inmost desires.
- You would like to be able to identify where God is present and active in your everyday experience.
- You are puzzled by what others mean when they say they heard "God's voice" or "God telling me."
- You have wondered about the division of labor between God and you in the decision-making process.
- You face a dilemma right now where you are wondering what faithfulness to God looks like.

If any of these statements resonate with you, I hope you will keep reading. My prayer is that, through my words, God will shed light on your way.

The question *What should I do?* is one we ask ourselves many times in one day! To find answers to the myriad choices we face daily about how we should live our lives, we can't just type each question into Google and expect to receive a wise response that applies specifically to us and our unique situation in the moment. If we truly want to know God's personal will for our lives, we must develop our capacity for discernment.

Ever since my initial surrender to Jesus Christ, the theme of discernment has been a close and constant companion. Soon after this commitment moment, I wanted to know God's personal will for my one life here on earth. While I knew that God's general will could be found in Scripture, I deeply desired to discover God's specific will for my life. This desire has never left me. Right now, as I enter my seventies, discerning how God is leading me for this season continues to be an important task. The ongoing journey of discernment has turned my life into an adventure of faith for which I will always be immeasurably grateful to God.

In the decades since becoming a Christ follower, I have learned a great deal about the process of discernment. God's personal will is not usually written in bold letters across the sky or printed on a sheet of paper dropped from heaven. It is something we learn to discern. Because our personal calling is dynamic, ever evolving, and always moment to moment, the quest to discern God's will is an ongoing adventure. In my own faith journey, I have been fortunate to meet some veterans of the Spirit who have taught me much about discernment. I would like to share these insights that I have learned with you in the hope that my words will help you live more faithfully and purposefully as a Christ follower within those places where you live and work.

I want to explore an understanding of God's personal will that does not diminish the importance of our responsibility in the process of discernment. God does not always tell us what to do! God intends us to grow and mature into grown-up children of God. This involves learning how to explore options, making life-giving decisions, and taking responsibility for our actions. Character only develops as we learn to do this. Discerning what God wants, therefore, involves paying careful attention to what God is doing and saying *and* to what we think and feel about the choices we are facing.

## Hoped-For Outcomes

I have three hopes for you as a reader and a fellow pilgrim. First, I hope to offer you an inviting, accessible, and compelling vision of God's personal will for your life. One of the most exciting truths of our faith is that each of us is called by name by God. This God-shaped vocation goes far beyond working out what we must do with our lives. It also involves discovering what kind of person we are called to become. As we live into the truth of our uniqueness,

God moves us toward the fullness of life that Jesus promised. I hope that you will catch glimpses of what it may mean for you to become the person you were destined to be from eternity.

Second, I would like to develop for you a clear understanding of what I mean by "discernment." What does it mean to "discern God's personal will"? These words get used often in church circles. What meanings do we attach to them? As we journey together, I would like us to carefully create a biblically shaped imagination around them. A wise mentor once reminded me that we live at the mercy of our ideas. Certainly this is the case when it comes to our ideas about discernment. There is much at stake in this regard. Sadly, we can go through our whole life without becoming the person God created us to be. Alternatively, when we truly become who God wants us to be and express our true personhood, we are able to contribute more to the healing of our broken world.

Third, I would like us to explore *how* we can intentionally go about discerning God's personal will for our lives. A friend of mine, when he reads a book, often writes in the margins the letters *YBH*. When I asked him about what these letters stood for, he answered, "Yes, but how?" I hope that you will not need to write these letters in the margins of this book! Although discernment is certainly not a spiritual technique or a five-step plan, there are practices that can deepen our capacity to live discerningly. Throughout this book I will invite you to engage in these practices and discover their usefulness for yourself.

## How Best to Use This Book

I intend this book to be primarily a user's guide to discerning God's personal will for our lives. The reason is straightforward. Learning to discern is like learning to swim. We do not learn to swim by reading about swimming. We learn by getting into the water, having someone come alongside us to coach us, swallowing some water, sinking now and then, learning the different strokes, putting them to use, and discovering over time what swimming involves. As we practice our strokes, our ability to swim gets stronger and stronger.

It is the same with spiritual discernment. We learn to discern as we step into the unfathomable depths of God's love, ask the Holy Spirit to come alongside us, practice those discernment skills passed on to us by our sisters and brothers in the faith, reflect on those times when we sank underwater, and slowly discover what it means to trust the flow of God's loving will in our lives. This book has been designed to encourage you to do this. As the old proverb puts it, "Hear and forget; see and remember; do and understand."

For this reason, the discernment exercises throughout each chapter are the most important part of this book. These practices have been devised over the years as I have led courses and retreats on this theme of discerning God's personal will. This book is structured around these exercises. If you read this book without doing the exercises, it will be like standing at the side of the swimming pool and watching others swim but never swimming yourself. I hope I can encourage you to jump into the water!

This book can be used effectively in a group setting. It could be with fellow pilgrims from your local faith community, or an established small group, or simply a band of friends wanting to explore together what it means to discern God's personal will for each of your lives. If there is no such group available, I would strongly encourage you to find a partner with whom you can share your reflections as you read each chapter and engage with the discernment exercises. Our journey with Jesus should always involve others.

The best way to prepare for each meeting is to read the relevant chapter and do the suggested exercises beforehand. I have outlined a possible format for your group meeting so that you can share your learning from the week (see appendix 1). If you are unable to be part of a group or to discuss the material with a friend, my biggest encouragement is to read the book slowly, taking time to do the suggested exercises, and then perhaps make some notes in your journal.

## Journeying with Jesus

Jesus is the only person who perfectly discerned God's personal will. He alone became wholly the person his Father wanted him to be. He alone did fully what his Father wanted him to do. He alone fulfilled his Father's calling with total surrender and complete faithfulness. Most wonderfully, as we seek to discern God's personal will for our lives, he lives today beyond crucifixion as the risen Christ and offers to walk alongside us as our ever-loving Friend and Lord. We can be sure that as we turn to our living Lord and keep our hand in his, he will shed his bright light on our way, one step at a time.

*Trevor Hudson*

*Part One*

# INTRODUCING

# GOD'S

# WILL

# Chapter 1

# ANNOUNCING GOOD NEWS

*I am created to do something or to be something for which no one
else is created; I have a place in God's counsels, in God's world,
which no one else has; . . . God knows me and calls me by my name.*

JOHN HENRY NEWMAN

I read this profound saying: "God sends each person into this
world with a special message to deliver, with a special song to sing
for others, with a special act of love to bestow."[1] No one else can
speak my message, or sing my song, or offer my act of love. These
are entrusted only to me. Ever since I first read these words, they
have warmed my heart. They not only touch me; whenever I share
them, they resonate with others, too. Why is this?

One significant decision facing us all concerns the way we see
our little life in this big universe. This choice is stark. On the one
hand, do we see human life as simply random? Are we accidental
specks of dust in an ultimately meaningless cosmos? After all, there
are over eight billion of us—how can our one life really matter? On
the other hand, does our existence here on earth have a purpose?

Is there a unique space in this world where each of our lives is meant to shine? Do you and I have a specific purpose to fulfill in the years given to us?

The bottom line is that we either view our lives as meaningless or as brimming over with more meaning than we can imagine. Our ideas about these questions have life-shaping consequences.

Early in my twenties, I read *Man's Search for Meaning*, written by Jewish psychiatrist Viktor Frankl, who spent time in a concentration camp during the Second World War. He noticed something during his imprisonment that would shape his life's work. With his clinically trained eye, he observed that there were two groups of prisoners: those who just gave in to their horrific circumstances and those who lived through them with dignity and hope. As Frankl studied this second group, he noticed one common characteristic: They all had something meaningful to live for. In one unforgettable sentence, he underscored that the person "who has a *why* to live for can bear with almost any *how*."[2]

The astonishing good news that the Bible gives, as we will soon see, is that God has a personal will for each of us. Because we find this truth so hard to learn by heart, we need to hear it repeatedly. So let me repeat it to you right now:

> *You have been desired into existence by a Great Love. You are meant to be here. You are known by name. You have been chosen. You have been called by name. Your life has a unique, God-given meaning. Your unrepeatable life matters.*

When this good news reverberates in the depths of our soul, our small life takes on an eternal significance in God's great universe.

## Biblical Glimpses

The good news of God's personal will, or personal calling, weaves its way throughout the Bible. Let me offer you three brief glimpses.

1. In Psalm 139, we read, "It was you who formed my inward parts; you knit me together in my mother's womb. I praise you, for I am fearfully and wonderfully made" (verses 13-14). The psalmist reminds us that God has been creatively present in our lives from our very beginning. Each one of us has been uniquely, carefully, and marvelously made. You and I are not here by mistake. This astounding biblical truth opens our eyes to glimpse God's eternal intention for your life and mine.

   Let me take the psalmist's assertion one step further. God has not put down those creative knitting needles! Sometimes we imagine that once God gave us life, the Creator then stood back and said, "Okay, I have done my job, and from now on I will not be involved in your life anymore." Nothing could be further from the truth. Our creation is not just a past event. God continues to give life to you and me—and to the whole expanding universe. Right now, the great and glorious I AM continues to create us, breathing breath into our being, calling us to become the fully alive human God wants us to be.

2. God's personal will can be seen in that evocative biblical phrase *called by name*. One example can be found in John chapter 10, where we read that the Good Shepherd "calls his own sheep by name" (verse 3). We are known personally by God. You and I are not merely one in a crowd, or the product of an assembly line, or an anonymous statistic. The God who has created every one of the over eight billion people on this planet has a personal and unique name for each one of

us. This gospel conviction about the mystery of who we are invites our astonishment, careful reflection, and meditation.

In biblical times, names carried great significance. They were not just how people were addressed, which is the general purpose they serve today. They described the essence of a person's character. Your name was a description of who you were and what your parents hoped you would become. Similarly, the God whose loving heart we see in Jesus has a personal name for each of us. This is our true name, our deepest identity, our divine calling. God's will is that you and I discover this truth of our uniqueness. Each of us is born to be who we are, not copies of one another.

3. We get a glimpse of God's personal will in Paul's words in the New Testament. He repeatedly underlines the importance of discerning our personal calling. He implores the Christ followers in Rome to offer themselves to God and to let their minds be transformed so that they would discern "what is the will of God—what is good and acceptable and perfect" (Romans 12:2). Paul's letter to the Ephesians divides into two parts with his hinge verse challenging his readers "to lead a life worthy of the calling to which you have been called" (Ephesians 4:1). Writing to the Corinthian believers, he says emphatically, "Let each of you lead the life . . . to which God called you" (1 Corinthians 7:17).

This good news of God's personal will, or personal calling, runs throughout the New Testament. It proves false the idea that only certain people, like missionaries and ministers, are called by God. I remember going to my boss at Firestone in my early twenties to tell him that I was leaving to explore becoming a minister in the Methodist church.

He said to me, "Oh, so you are one of those who have been called." Even though I knew him to be a person of faith, he did not see himself as called. Often that is our understanding of how God works: God calls some people but not others. But that's not the case. The good news is that God has a specific purpose for every one of us, including you!

I hope you now have a clearer biblical understanding of God's personal will. On the one hand, God has a general will for how we are called to live. We witness this clearly in God's guidelines for human living revealed in the Scriptures. This divine guidance includes things like learning to love those around us, working for justice, walking humbly through life, offering hospitality to strangers, and living in the light. Consider, too, that often-overlooked phrase in Jesus' great commission where he expressed his intention for us to obey everything that he had taught us (Matthew 28:20).

On the other hand, God's personal will involves discovering how all this takes shape in your life and mine—and this will look different for every Christ follower. It is about discovering the message that we are called to deliver, the song that we are called to sing, and that special act of love that we alone can give. No one else can convey our message, sing our song, or do our act of love. These are entrusted to us alone. This is our personal calling from God. It has two important dimensions that we will explore now: becoming the person God wants us to be and doing the works God wants us to do.

## Becoming the Person God Wants Us to Be

Each one of us is called to live the truth of our unrepeatable uniqueness. We are not meant to model ourselves after others, however wonderful they may be. A delightful Jewish parable makes this point. When Rabbi Eleazar died and arrived in heaven, as the legend goes, he was worried about his degree of holiness. He wondered whether God was going to be angry with him. He imagined God cross-questioning him about his way of life, saying, "Tell me, why did you not become like Abraham, the man of faith, or like Moses, the man of action?" However, when God approached the rabbi, the question was altogether different. "Tell me, my son," asked God quietly, "why did you not become Rabbi Eleazar?"[3]

Becoming the person God wants us to be is not as simple as it sounds. Certainly it has not been for me. Getting along in this world often means pretending to be who we are not. We wear masks that reflect how we want others to see us. We pretend to have it all together when we are really falling apart inside. We say that we are fine when we are struggling. We give the impression that we are strong when we feel fragile. We try to look brave when we are scared. We cover feelings of resentment with a veneer of niceness. In the end, we move further and further away from the person God wants us to be until we cannot distinguish between the masks we put on and who we really are.

In the chapters that follow, we will learn to discern how we can grow more fully into the person God wants us to be. As a starting point for this lifelong pilgrimage, here is a simple framework to guide us.[4] I have found it helpful to recognize that we each have three selves. As we bring them all to God, a gradual transformation begins taking place within us. We begin to show up as the person God wants us to be. We embrace God's personal will for our lives.

- First, there is our *external self.* This is the self that we show to the world. It gets communicated through how we speak, what we say or do not say about ourselves, how we dress, how we carry ourselves, the words we use, and so forth. This external self is not necessarily false; it often helps us carry out our responsibilities in the world. We cannot always wear our heart on our sleeve. However, we need to be careful that too big a gap does not develop between this external self and what is happening inside us. We feel discomfort when people say affirming things about us that we know are not true. Identifying ourselves completely with this external self exposes us to the dangers of self-deception and blocks us from becoming the person God wants us to be.

- Second, there is our *present self*. Each of us was uniquely created by God in our mother's womb. This present self consists of our fears, our pain, our tears, our childhood wounds, our longings, our gifts, our resentments, our betrayals, our competitiveness, and our powerful instinctual drives. All this lies a little beneath the surface of our lives. Sometimes we consciously hide these parts from others. I think especially of those powerful secret drives of our sexuality and aggression. While both are God-given with tremendous potential for good, these drives are often forced into hiding, with sometimes tragic consequences.

- Third, there is our *becoming self*. The good news of our faith is that, as we bring to God what we know about ourselves, God slowly knits together all the various threads of our lives into the unique person God wants us to be. In this way we cooperate with God in the ongoing transformation of our heart and mind into God's family likeness. Using the language of Paul, we are working out our salvation "with fear and trembling" (Philippians 2:12). Each of us has hidden within us the wondrous beauty of a personality that God wants us to shine forth for the sake of others.

This transformative journey involves a courageous honesty to acknowledge and accept who we really are, to share who we are with trusted companions, and to let God's Spirit birth that unique, loving person we were created to be.

---

### Discernment Exercise

*You can begin this transforming journey right now. Here are some simple steps: Know that you are infinitely precious to God, who always delights in you. Give thanks to God for the hidden mystery of your being. Reflect on that gap between the external self you show to those around you and your present self, with all its light and darkness. Put your arms around all the beautiful, bruised, and broken bits of your life. Celebrate the good news that you are known, loved, and accepted by God in Christ as you are. Remind yourself that you do not need to pretend in the company of the Divine Presence. Offer all of yourself to the Compassionate One, who longs to welcome you. Give consent to the Holy Spirit, who wants to help you become fully yourself. Repeat this practice often as you embark on this discerning journey into God's personal will for your life.*

---

## Doing the Works God Wants Us to Do

Many years ago, I watched a documentary on the remarkable ministry of Mother Teresa among the poverty-stricken people of Calcutta. At one stage there was a moving exchange between her and the commentator. He asked her whether she did not find her work futile and hopeless given the immensity of human need facing her and her sisters. In her typically humble fashion, she responded, "I was not called to be successful but faithful. Each one of us is called to do something beautiful for God."[5]

You are not alone if you struggle to believe this. Often, we feel our smallness. We are filled with self-doubt and have little sense of how we can play our part in God's big dream of healing this broken world. So when someone like Mother Teresa suggests that each of us has something beautiful to accomplish in our lifetime, we are only half convinced. Yet there are specific works that God wants each one of us to do. Consider these words written by Paul to the Ephesians: "We are God's handiwork, created in Christ Jesus to do good works, which God prepared in advance for us to do" (Ephesians 2:10, NIV).

This is a wonderfully challenging verse. It reminds us that God has good works for each of us to do. These are intimately connected to how, as God's creative handiwork, we have been knitted together in our mother's womb. God's personal will is that you and I live out our little piece of God's dream for this world, with actions that fit the shape of our being. This outward journey in serving those around us is intimately linked with our inward journey to become the person God wants us to be. Becoming who we were created to be, we find ourselves doing those works God wants us to do. Or, putting it the other way 'round, discovering what we are called to do introduces us to who we truly are.

This life-giving insight from Paul's letter is motivating. Many voices try to tell us what to do, how to live, and what goals we must set. Some of these voices can be helpful. Many of us have received help from significant others who have called forth our gifts, expressed appreciation when we have done something well, and encouraged us to step out beyond our comfort zones. I will always be grateful to the mentors in my life who encouraged me to write, even though I found the prospect quite daunting and overwhelming. Without their support and challenge, I would not have written.

However, if the shape of our life is *defined* by these voices, we may neglect what we know deep down in our heart we are called to do. We can easily end up living from the outside in and not from the inside out. The consequences are sad. We live reactively rather than responsively. We experience an absence of meaning in what we are doing. Our lives are shaped by others' expectations rather than by any sense of doing what God wants us to do. We seldom listen to the quiet whispers of our own hearts. Saddest of all is that we forget we were created to be different, with a specific calling that no other human being can fulfill for us. We miss God's personal will.

Thankfully, it does not have to always be this way. We can choose—*right now*—to open our heart and mind to the good news that God has good works in mind for each of us to do. You have something beautiful to do for God, and so do I. These special assignments express who we have been uniquely created to be. Few things are more important than taking this challenge seriously. We are never too old to begin this quest and to discover what these good works may look like in our life.

### Discernment Exercise

*We can start discerning God's personal will wherever we are right now. Here is an exercise you may like to try. Make a list of all your tasks, responsibilities, and roles. Write down your feelings and thoughts about each one. (You may have both positive and negative feelings about the same activity.) Be as honest as you can. Which of these activities seem to express who you are? Which of them seem to conflict with who you are? Which make you feel more alive? Which deaden your spirit? You may find it helpful to talk this over with God and to listen to what God may be saying to you.*

## Fullness of Life

God's will for each of us is fullness of life. This includes showing up in this world as the person God wants us to be. It is about discovering our lines while we are on the stage of our one life. It is about delivering our special message, singing our special song, and bestowing our special act of love. It is about discerning the *why* to our existence so we can face the hard realities of our lives with hope, courage, and dignity. There may be no greater tragedy than going through our lives and totally missing this. But we are alive right now, so let us respond to the good news that God has a personal calling for each one of us by discerning it day by day, beginning now.

# Chapter 2

# UNDERSTANDING DISCERNMENT

*Practicing discernment is essential to the spiritual life.*

DENISE ACKERMANN

Let me begin this chapter by saying to you,

> *You have been loved into existence by God. You are known, chosen, and called by name. Your life counts. God wants you to live life in all its fullness. There is an unrepeatable purpose for your being here on earth. No one else will ever be in the space that you occupy in time and place. Your divine calling is to become the unique person you are meant to be and to do those unique tasks that have your name written on them.*[1]

I hope you will let these words settle in your heart and mind. Our little life here on this earth has more significance than we could ever imagine. Over the years, it has been profoundly moving to watch people take this astonishing good news seriously. I have witnessed that when they begin to explore God's personal will for their own lives, they receive strength to avoid despair and hopelessness, even in the toughest times. I pray that you will come to know this for yourself in your own experience.

Once we realize that God has a specific intention for our life, our immediate response is usually "Yes, but how do I know what God wants for my life?" The key is *discernment*. God does not phone us telling us precisely who we must become and what we must do. We must take the time and make the effort to discern who God wants us to be and what God wants us to do. This does not happen automatically. Our personal calling is discerned in an ongoing, intentional process that happens within our conscious relationship with God.

Before I describe discernment, I want to respond to a few concerns that sometimes get expressed about the need for discernment.

## Why Discern?

Many Christians believe discernment is unnecessary. "Everything we need to know about God's will," they say, "is in the Bible." As I underlined in the previous chapter, God's general will for us *is* expressed on the pages of Scripture. The Bible tells us that we are called to love God and our neighbor, live in the light, work for justice, seek reconciliation, be hospitable toward strangers, be faithful in our commitments, and do as much good as possible. However, the crucial question always remains: How do these broad biblical guidelines from God find practical expression within the particulars of our daily life?

There are also many life situations where the Bible does not specifically tell us what to do. It does not tell us what career to follow, what job offer to accept, whom to marry, where to reside, which degree to pursue, when to retire, which human need to address, whether to emigrate, which political party to vote for—and the list goes on and on. In these kinds of decision moments, we must discern how we can best move forward in faith, hope, and love. The responsibility to discern how God is leading us in our next step always involves reflection and prayer.

Others believe that discernment is unnecessary because their pastor, or their church's teachings, or the pope will tell them what they must do. Again, I respond carefully. As people of faith, we belong to faith communities where we are accountable to leadership. Their guidance is important. We do not follow Jesus in an isolated bubble. We have sisters and brothers who give us wisdom and shed light on the decisions we must make. But the need for personal discernment persists. If we do not take our responsibility to discern seriously, we fail to grow up into adult children of God, and we will remain immature in our faith journey, always needing someone else to tell us what to do.

Some resist discernment because they believe "you will just know what the Spirit wants you to do." As a young Christ follower, I was often intimidated by people of faith who would confidently pepper their conversations with "The Lord told me . . ." Somehow it just never seemed that clear for me. Anyway, the results of this approach to knowing God's will have not always been convincing. When I was a young probationer minister, someone dropped off a pair of shoes for me because "the Lord had told them to do it." When I tried them on, they did not fit! I began to wonder whether the Lord knows my shoe size.

Discerning God's leading does not undermine the activity of the Spirit. Rather, the opposite is true. We need to discern

God's personal will because the movement of the Spirit is usually quiet, hidden, and subtle. The Spirit does not take the gift of our God-given freedom away from us. In God's individual dealings with us, God always gives us room for initiative, risk taking, and responsibility—and even for failure, uncertainty, and imperfection! This is how we grow more mature and adventurous in our faith and how we have a freer walk with God. Our efforts to discern how the Spirit is guiding us express our longing to be faithful to what God wants for our lives and to follow God's lead purposefully.

On the pages that follow, I will do my best to offer an understanding of discernment that takes seriously both God's specific leadings *and* our thoughtful cooperation. Here are three introductory thoughts to get us started. As Christ followers attempting to discern God's personal will for us, each of us is called to

- recognize God's active presence in all things,
- listen to the Divine Whisper, and
- keep God's big dream alive.

Let's look at each of these invitations in turn.

## Recognizing God's Active Presence in All Things

As we begin to describe discernment, we must overcome our tendency to live with a split spirituality. This happens when we divide our lives into two spheres: the spiritual and the nonspiritual. Into the first sphere we place those "religious" activities like praying, Bible reading, worshiping, and church activities. Into the second sphere we place those "nonreligious" activities relating to health, sexuality, relationships, studies, leisure moments, crises, politics, economics, and so on.

When we separate our everyday living like this, we confine God to the first so-called spiritual sphere, with the tragic result that the work of discernment gets cut off from most of the activities of our actual lives.

This tendency is more widespread than you may think. It often gets expressed in how we pray and speak. Think about the things we pray about and those we leave out. We wrongly believe that God is only interested in certain parts of our lives and not others. Here is a simple test: How often do you share with God struggles with sexuality, choices about what to spend money on, challenges at work, conflicts in relationships, dilemmas regarding the inequalities that surround us, and so on? I cannot count the times someone has said to me after I have preached, "Thank you so much for the message. But now it is back to the real world." Notice the underlying assumption that God is present and active in our "church space" but not in our "real-life space."

The biblical witness to how God relates to us is radically different. It teaches us that God's active presence is in every experience, every encounter, and every event. There is no place in our everyday lives where God is not present or at work. God's divine fingerprints are everywhere. Consider these words from Psalm 139:

Where can I go from your Spirit?
    Where can I flee from your presence?
If I go up to the heavens, you are there;
    if I make my bed in the depths, you are there.
If I rise on the wings of the dawn,
    if I settle on the far side of the sea,

even there your hand will guide me,
　　your right hand will hold me fast.

PSALM 139:7-10, NIV

The Boundless Mystery we call God is continuously at work in the life of every one of us. In everything that happens to us, God is always seeking to draw us—and all creation—into greater fullness of life.

This truth can be traced throughout the New Testament. Preaching on Mars Hill, Paul stressed that the God we worship "does not live in temples built by human hands"; rather, *in God* "we live and move and have our being" (Acts 17:24, 28, NIV). Later, in his letter to the Ephesians, he proclaimed that there is "one God and Father of all, who is over all and through all and in all" (Ephesians 4:6, NIV). A few sentences later, referring to the risen and ascended Christ, Paul explained that he fills "the whole universe" (Ephesians 4:10, NIV). And in Jesus' last words recorded by Matthew, we read that he said to his disciples, "Surely I am with you always, to the very end of the age" (Matthew 2(ceb8:20, NIV).

How does this conviction about God's active presence in all things relate to discernment? Simply this: Discernment is required in every aspect of our lives. When we seek to discern God's personal will for us, we must consider matters relating to worship, personal devotions, times of fellowship, and family devotions as well as relationships, work, finances, leisure, nature, technology, politics, and so much else. This process involves recognizing God's presence and activity in every part of our lives, and in the world around us, and discerning how God wants us to respond. It means bringing the whole of our lives into harmony with God's ever-present activity—wherever we are and whatever we are doing.

<hr>

### Discernment Exercise

*Where do we begin? Our starting point is to look at what is happening within and around us right now. How may God be nudging us to move toward greater truthfulness, honesty, and reality in who we are and how we behave? How may God be inviting us to choose life rather than death in our present relationships at home and work? What actions of compassionate helpfulness have our name written on them that will bring life to us and those around us? Speaking with God about wonderings like these opens the way for us to bring our daily lives in tune with how God is at work within and around us. Why don't you take a few minutes to reflect on this now?*

<hr>

## Listening to the Divine Whisper

The God we meet in the pages of Scripture is the God who speaks. Here are two of my favorite passages about God speaking. In 1 Kings 19, we read of the prophet Elijah's flight into the desert. He was terrified that Queen Jezebel was going to kill him, and he ran for his life. Eventually he arrived at Mount Horeb, where he spent forty days and nights. There he was told to stand on the mountain, "for the LORD is about to pass by" (verse 11, NIV). There came a great and powerful wind, then an earthquake, then a fire. But God was not in any of these. Finally, after all these spectacular events subsided and there was silence, we read that God spoke to Elijah in "a gentle whisper" (verse 12, NIV).

My other favorite passage about God speaking is about Jesus, the Good Shepherd, and is found in John 10. Already we have noted how Jesus tells us that he "calls his own sheep by name" (verse 3, NIV). In this same verse, he says that his sheep "listen to his voice" (also see verse 27, NIV). The lovely picture here is of the Good Shepherd going ahead of his flock, calling each sheep by name. The sheep follow *because they know his voice*. The implication is clear: Jesus, who now lives beyond crucifixion, has not stopped speaking. He comes alongside us as our Risen Shepherd and invites us to learn to listen for his voice. As we heed his voice, he leads and guides us along our way into the fullness of life that he offers us.

Throughout history Christ followers have attested to this truth. Saint Augustine, that great African saint from the fifth century, prayed longingly for God to "whisper words of truth in [his] heart, for you alone speak truth."[2] In one of our hymns, Charles Wesley joyfully celebrated the risen Jesus, who "speaks, and listening to his voice . . . the humble poor believe."[3] Mother Teresa encouraged her readers "to listen to God because it's not what we say but what He says to us and through us that matters."[4] Unquestionably for these giants in the faith, and for others who share a similar testimony, God is Someone who speaks to us personally.

Listening to the God who speaks is crucial if we want to discern God's personal will. The two are inseparable. Jesus is our supreme example. For him, listening to his Abba Father's voice lay at the heart of his ministry. He was surrounded by many voices—those coming from his Jewish heritage, the religious authorities, the Roman government, his disciples, the crowds around him, and even the evil one. Yet the one voice that defined his understanding of who he was called to be and what he was called to do was the voice of the One who had sent him. Perhaps this is the reason why, when I asked a wise friend what one thing mattered most as I sought to discern God's will in a difficult vocational moment, he answered quietly, "Listen to the Divine Whisper."

Now, I am aware as I write these words that they will raise

many questions. *What do you mean by the "Divine Whisper"? What does the voice of the Good Shepherd sound like? How does God speak to us today? How do we know when it is God speaking and not just our own thoughts? Are there reliable criteria for discerning the voice of the Spirit?* These are critical questions, and we will pay careful attention to them, especially in chapters 4 and 9.

## Discernment Exercise

*Take some time now to allow the biblical witness to the speaking God, and the testimony of other Christ followers, to sink deeply into your heart and mind. Here are some striking words from Donald Coggan that may help you do this: "Christians believe in a God who speaks. Ours is not a silent God, a God who sits, Sphinx-like, looking out unblinking on a world in agony.... [God] speaks because he loves. Love always seeks to communicate."⁵ What are your thoughts and feelings about this bold testimony to the God who wants to lovingly communicate with us? Share them honestly with God and listen for how God may respond.*

## Keeping God's Big Dream Alive

God has not only a personal will for your life and mine but also a huge dream for our world. We catch glimpses of this dream in the biblical prophecies. Here are two prophetic images that catch my imagination:

> They shall beat their swords into plowshares,
> and their spears into pruning hooks;
> nation shall not lift up sword against nation,
> neither shall they learn war anymore.

ISAIAH 2:4, esv

The wolf shall live with the lamb,
>   the leopard shall lie down with the kid. . . .
They will not hurt or destroy
>   on all my holy mountain;
for the earth will be full of the knowledge of the LORD
>   as the waters cover the sea.

ISAIAH 11:6, 9

Can you imagine what this kind of world would look like in real-life terms?

It is not easy to keep God's big dream in front of us. It gets mocked by loud voices that shout, "In this world, it is every person for themself! If you do not look after yourself, no one else will. You must push, shove, and climb over those around you so that you stay ahead of the pack. It is a pipe dream to think that we can live together as members of one family." These messages usually take the place of God's intention for our world in our heart and mind. The consequences are sad. Rather than living in harmony with God's dream, we live a self-centered and fearful life that builds walls instead of bridges between people.

Jesus challenges us to keep God's dream alive. He has taught us to pray, "Your kingdom come, your will be done, on earth as it is in heaven" (Matthew 6:10, ESV). He wants us to share God's intention for this world so that our choices would be in tune with it. Discernment enters the picture again.

Each day we get confronted with many choices, some trivial and others more substantial, about how we will choose to live in the public spaces of our life. As Christ followers, how are we going to pray *and* live the Lord's Prayer? Or to put it differently, how do we discern our little part in God's big dream so that we can make it more real where we live and work? God's purposes for our wounded world will only move forward as you and I discern how we can more faithfully cooperate with them, wherever we are.

God's personal will for our lives always connects with God's general will for the world. When we begin to deliver our special message, sing our special song, and bestow our special act of love, we find ourselves drawn more deeply into God's immense dream. We discover that our true happiness lies in living in tune with what God wants for the whole universe. As E. Stanley Jones, that great Methodist missionary, wrote, "The most miserable people in the world are the people who are self-centered, who don't do anything for anybody, except themselves. They are centers of misery with no exception. . . . On the contrary, the happiest people are the people who deliberately take on themselves the sorrows and troubles of others. Their hearts sing with a strange wild joy."[6]

### Discernment Exercise

*You may like to put this book down for a moment and think about God's big dream for our world. Let it stir your heart to want to make it more real where you live and work. Right now, God is actively present in all things, working in hidden ways to bring about what God longs for. God wants you to become a friend and partner in making this divine dream a greater reality. God invites you to play your part in making this universe a more harmonious, friendly, and life-giving place for all—at home, at work, at church, in the community—in all that we do. Spend some time now sharing with God your feelings and thoughts about this divine invitation.*

## A Simple Description

As we end this chapter, I want to draw together my three thoughts about discernment in a simple description of this critical practice:

> *Discernment is learning to recognize God's active presence and to listen to God's voice so that we may bring our lives into harmony with what God wants for us and play our part in keeping God's big dream for the world alive.*

If your appetite to know God's personal will for your life has been whetted, why don't you ask God to give you this gift of discernment? After all, you have been called by name!

*Part Two*

# DISCERNING

# GOD'S

# WILL

*Chapter 3*

# ALIGNING OUR HEART WITH
# THE HEART OF GOD

*Christian surrender is saying yes to God's Yes! to me.*

DAVID BENNER

Let us explore the first step in discerning God's personal will. When we wake up to the good news that we are called by name, a longing is born within us to know *how* we can discover this personal calling that God has in mind for each one of us.

Our journey of discernment starts as we align our heart with God's heart. This starting point finds support in the words that Paul wrote to the Christ followers in Rome: "I appeal to you therefore, brothers and sisters, by the mercies of God, to present your bodies as a living sacrifice, holy and acceptable to God, which is your spiritual worship. Do not be conformed to this world, but be transformed by the renewing of your minds, so that you may discern what is the will of God—what is good and acceptable and perfect" (Romans 12:1-2).

The message is clear. As we surrender to God in response to what God has done for us, we place ourselves in a position to discern God's guidance and leading.

This starting point must be underlined: Something is missing in our relationship with God if we only connect when we need guidance. Imagine a relationship with someone in which they only call you when they want something. For the rest of the time, they show no interest in you whatsoever. They are not interested in what you like, what you value, or what you think or feel. When a tough time comes along, however, you are the one they call. They phone, ask for advice, and want immediate guidance. How would you feel about this situation? What would you think? This is not the kind of relationship God wants with us.

More critically, aligning our heart with God's is a nonnegotiable prerequisite for discerning God's leadings. Think for a moment of your most intimate relationship. You only get to know your partner's or close friend's heart when you spend time together, pay attention to each other, and give yourselves to one another. As the intimacy between you deepens, your awareness of what she or he wants becomes clearer. Something similar happens in our relationship with God. Discerning God's personal will assumes living in an ever-deepening intimacy with our Divine Friend. It is almost impossible to know how God is calling us when we are not living in tune with God.

---

### Discernment Exercise

*I hope you have seen that discernment is a relational matter. We become more sensitive and responsive to divine leading as our intimacy with God deepens. So let me ask you: Are you willing to explore what it means to get your heart in tune with the heart of God? Are you open to letting go of whatever attachments and attitudes get in the way of this alignment? Are you ready to take the risks that intimate relationships always invite? Are you willing to allow God's active and living presence to fill you? If your answer to these questions is yes, you are ready to embark on the adventure of discerning God's personal will for your life.*

---

## Our Picture of God

We will only choose to align our heart with God's when we know—in our inmost being—that we are deeply loved by God.

Many of us do not believe this. We feel that God is against us, or not interested in us, or angry with us. When we carry this negative picture of God around with us, we will probably relate to God in a formal way rather than in the way of an intimate, personal friendship. So let me ask you: What do you honestly believe God feels toward you?

It was in a time of emotional desperation, nearly forty years ago, that I needed to come to terms with what I believed God felt about me. I was sitting with a psychiatrist in his office at a Johannesburg hospital. I was in a space of personal despair, overwhelming weariness, and doubt about my calling. For over an hour I shared the struggles of my soul, my tiredness in body, and my distance from God. Dr. Allwood listened carefully, and when I had finished, he asked me a surprising question: "Trevor, what is your picture of God?" Clearly, he saw connections between my inner turmoil, my spiritual fatigue, and my view of God that I was not able to make.

That question began a journey of exploration. For the first time I reflected on my image of God. I discovered that I saw God as Someone whose love and affirmation needed to be earned. Even though I preached about God's unconditional acceptance, my default belief was that I needed to measure up to God's expectations to receive it. This deeply ingrained way of relating to God translated into how I related to those around me, as if acceptance and love are earned through performance. You do not need to be a psychiatrist to see how this flawed view of God lay at the root of my drained emotional and spiritual condition.

The healing of my negative picture of God continues even today. What has helped me most is to look at God through the words and life of Jesus again and again. Think of Jesus' description of how the father welcomed his prodigal son home: "While he was still a long way off, his father saw him and was filled with compassion for him; he ran to his son, threw his arms around him and kissed him" (Luke 15:20, NIV). Divine compassion fills the whole being of God. There is no room for anything else. Like the sun that constantly shines, so God's love radiates toward us continually, whether we receive that love or not. Getting to know this Great Love has gradually moved from just being an idea in my head to a personal knowing in my heart.

This journey from the head to the heart has not been straightforward and is not over by any means. It often feels like taking two steps forward and one step back. When I feel I have failed God, it is easy for me to slip back into my default view. Rather than immediately coming back home and delighting in the welcoming embrace of Abba Father, my spontaneous response often is to think that God is disappointed in me. I feel I have let God down, and I begin to doubt whether God still loves me. Small wonder that one of my most frequent prayers goes, *Lord, please help me know your personal love more deeply.*

Nothing encourages us more to align our heart with God's than knowing we are unconditionally loved by God. So will you open your mind and heart more fully to this Great Love? When you accept your acceptance from God in Christ, your desire for intimacy with God will grow. You will want to discern who God wants you to be, and what God desires for your life, because you will be confident that God only ever wants the best for you. Coming to know for yourself that God is *for* you, and not against you, releases glorious possibilities for living in friendship with God. If you have a negative default picture of God, let the Holy Spirit change it. You can begin this heart journey now.

### *Discernment Exercise*

*One of the best ways to begin discerning God's personal love for you is to meditate on Jesus' parables. Start with his three parables in Luke 15. They show us that God is deeply interested in each one of us, even when we have messed up. Pay special attention to the shepherd who looks for the lost sheep and then to the woman who searches for her lost coin. Watch how they search, and imagine the feelings of their hearts, especially their joy and delight when they find what they are looking for. Last, in the parable of the prodigal son, picture the waiting father—watch his actions, listen to his words, empathize with how he feels. This is how our Divine Parent feels about us when we turn our back on our true home in God.*

*Meditating on these parables again and again can gradually change our faulty image of God. Slowly we begin to realize that nothing we can do could ever stop God from loving us and reaching out for us.*

## Surrendering to God

We align our heart with God's when we surrender our life and our will to God.

I use the word *surrender* carefully. Surrendering to God does not mean abdicating responsibility for our life, nor does it mean passively resigning ourselves to whatever happens. Certainly it does not mean becoming a doormat and allowing others to walk over us. As we come to know God's personal love, we come to see just how valuable our one life is. We realize that, because our life is a precious gift, we need to take responsibility for it and develop it in every way possible. We can only truly surrender ourselves to God when we have a real life to surrender, broken and imperfect as it may be.

My favorite biblical example of surrender is Mary. Recall that moment when the angel came to this young Jewish girl, greeted her warmly, and said to her that she would give birth to the Messiah. Imagine the shattering effects that announcement would have had on her. She was looking forward to marrying Joseph, settling down to village life in Nazareth, and raising a family. Suddenly her whole world was turned upside down. Bewildered, she cried out, "How can this be, since I am a virgin?" (Luke 1:34). When the angel told Mary that the Holy Spirit would come upon her, she responded freely, "Here am I, the servant of the Lord; let it be with me according to your word" (Luke 1:38).

Reflect for a few moments on her words. They describe powerfully what it means to surrender our life and our will to God. Mary was willing to let the God of all creation be God in her life. She submitted herself wholeheartedly to God's will for her future. She put God's purposes for her life ahead of her own. She consented to the presence and activity of the Spirit within her. When I think of Mary's moment of surrender, I think of opening hands. Rather than clenching her fists and saying no to God, she opened her hands and said yes. Through her act of surrender, she aligned her heart with God's heart.

This inner surrender only becomes possible when we know that God loves us without terms and conditions. Mary surrendered the way she did because she knew God loved her, would always be with her, and knew what was best. Can you see now why our picture of God is so critical? We will not freely surrender ourselves to someone we cannot trust or someone who does not love us. We will keep that person at a distance and make sure they do not have too much influence on our lives. In contrast, when we soak ourselves in God's relentless love toward us, expressed so clearly in Jesus Christ, we discover that our clenched fists can become open hands far more easily.

At the risk of oversimplifying things, there are two groups of people in the world. On the one hand are those whose hearts and minds are focused away from God's love. They have little interest in what God wants for their lives. They want to be their own boss. Their lives are curved inward, on *their* needs and what *they* want. They will never pray, *Your will be done.* Rather, they insist, "My will be done" or "I will do it my own way, thank you." These people have no interest in discerning God's personal will and most certainly will tragically miss out on discovering what God wants for their lives.

On the other hand are those who give themselves to God's love in simple trust and surrender. They are keenly interested in what God wants for them. What matters most for them is seeking and doing God's will. They want God to be at the center of their life. While they have thoughts and feelings about how they would like their life to go, they are more concerned about the way God wants them to travel through life. It could be said that written across their hearts is Jesus' prayer *Abba Father, your will be done.* These people end up knowing the joy of becoming the person God wants them to be and doing the works God wants them to do. They discover God's personal will for them and lead a life of faithfulness and purpose.

---

### Discernment Exercise

*How do you honestly feel about "surrendering yourself to God's love"? What thoughts come into your mind when you read this phrase? Take time to share these feelings and thoughts with God. What do you need from God to be able to surrender yourself more freely and with less struggle and strain? Could it be that you need to know more deeply that God loves and accepts you with no strings attached? Ask for the grace that you need from God that would help you say, with Mary, "Here am I... let it be with me according to your word."*

---

## Daily Surrender

We align our heart with God's when we choose to surrender daily.

Surrendering ourselves to God is not a once-and-for-all decision. It is an ongoing experience that continues throughout our days. I can surrender myself to God first thing in the morning, and then, when a crisis comes along, immediately take my life back again. We need to let our capacity for surrender permeate our whole being. This does not happen overnight. It is a journey that lasts our whole life. It involves continually exploring what surrender means within our daily relationships, roles, and responsibilities. Day after day, as we soak ourselves ever more deeply in God's loving acceptance, we turn our lives over to God with whatever trust and confidence we have.

Let me share some personal lessons about what this journey may look like. To begin with, aligning our heart with God's involves a conscious act of daily surrender. Every day brings with it an invitation to surrender ourselves anew to God, to entrust ourselves to God, and to let God be God in our lives. We need to be practical about this action and surround it with prayer. It is helpful to find a few moments at the beginning of the day to think about the coming day and consciously offer it to God. We can say a short prayer when we need to do something time sensitive or are faced with some problem. We can remind ourselves that we are not in control of everything that happens. If we have concerns for the day ahead, we can surrender them specifically to God and then do our best and trust God with the outcomes.

Learning to surrender daily also means accepting those difficult situations that cannot be changed. These may vary in seriousness from being stuck in traffic to devasting life experiences like being laid off or being diagnosed with a terminal illness or losing someone we love dearly. Events like these unmask the illusion that we are in complete control of what happens. We can either resist these unwelcome events and live with constant frustration and anger, or we can learn to accept them with God's help and grace. Accepting these unwanted intrusions can become the gateway to discerning how God wants us to live within them.

As one example, COVID restrictions made it impossible for my marriage partner, Debbie, and me to visit our children and grandchildren overseas. This unwelcome circumstance was difficult to accept. It brought much sadness and longing. Yet there was no way this situation could be changed. It could only be accepted. This meant facing my feelings of sadness and longing, welcoming them into my life rather than resisting or avoiding them, and then releasing them into God's care, again and again. This way of surrender helped me live through this painful time with a measure of joy and kept my heart open to what God's personal will for me involved.

Let me share one more lesson I am learning about daily surrender. It concerns the way we relate to others. Daily we encounter people who express views opposite to our own, hold values with which we cannot identify, and behave in ways different from how we live. Sometimes this can happen in our closest relationships. Often we want to straighten the other person out, fix them up, and tell them what they need to do. When they do not cooperate, we may get angry and frustrated. If we are wise, it will begin to dawn on us that we really cannot change other people. What we can do is to entrust them to God, show them our care without trying to change them, and accept them as they are. Surrendering ourselves to God means releasing others to God as well.

I remember my daughter, Joni, going to London on her own as an eighteen-year-old to listen to her favorite punk rock bands. I couldn't sleep for three nights because of my anxiety! On the one hand, I wanted to express my love and care for her. On the other hand, I knew I needed to give her the space to become the person she wanted to be. Amid my internal struggles, I wrote her these words. I also gave them to my son when he turned eighteen.

> I believe that you were created to live freely. I place your life in the loving hands of your Creator. I let go of my clinging hold of your life. I am willing for you to make your own choices. I no longer want to play god in your life. I will not believe that I always know what is best for your life. I want you to live your life according to your best understanding and light. I respect the image of God in you. I want to learn to love you with open hands. I love you, and I bless you. I have confidence in you and always will.

We need to hear the invitation to daily surrender repeatedly. We should not feel bad about this. Nor do we have to struggle and strain to yield ourselves to God. When we take our lives back into our hands, the best thing to do is to keep focused on the relentless love of God streaming toward us in Jesus Christ. This Perfect Love accepts us at whatever level of surrender we may be and draws us into an ever-deepening yielding of ourselves to God. It gives us strength to lay down whatever makes surrender hard for us and encourages us to open our hands toward God and say, with Mary again, "Here am I, the servant of the Lord; let it be with me according to your word."

## Discernment Exercise

*Sit comfortably before God with your palms facing up. In your imagination, place in your hands whatever blocks you from surrendering yourself wholeheartedly to God. Then turn your palms over so that they face downward. Picture yourself releasing those obstacles and moving into a deeper and fuller yielding of your life to God. Take your time as you do this. Last, turn your palms upward again as an expression of your openness to receiving God's love and mercy.*

## Embracing Surrender

I hope that you have caught a glimpse of how ongoing surrender brings our heart into alignment with the heart of God. Surrender is a deep inner act of saying yes to God, again and again, that opens our lives to God's active and living presence. We begin to want what God wants for us. We give up our willfulness, let go of the illusion of control over our own lives, and abandon ourselves into God's loving hands. We make room for the Good Shepherd to go before us, lead us, and guide us along our way. We become more responsive to the Divine Whisper prompting us about what to do next. We live in the flow of God's Spirit. Most wonderfully, we begin to discern God's personal will for our lives.

# Chapter 4

# LISTENING TO GOD IN SCRIPTURE

*Thus, if we read Scripture as we must, invoking the Holy Spirit,
what we encounter in Scripture is that living Word.*

ROWAN WILLIAMS

How do you pray? Most of us find it easier to talk to God than to listen to God. If we intend to live a life of discernment, this needs to change. Learning to listen to God and discerning the personal will of God go together. We'll struggle to discern how God wants us to live, especially within the nitty-gritty of daily life, if we do not learn to hear what God is saying to us here and now. Is this why the psalmist says, "*Today*, if you hear his voice . . ." (Psalm 95:7, ESV, emphasis added)? Listening is something we must always do in the present.

The importance of listening in our life of faith cannot be over-emphasized. Imagine any relationship where one person speaks all the time and the other person just listens. Such a relationship would be experienced as one-sided, insensitive, even boring. Yet this is how we often relate to God. Certainly, for almost the first ten years in my own relationship with God, prayer meant mostly talking to God. I seldom took time to listen. I simply did not know how.

Over time I have come to see that listening lies at the heart of our friendship with God. Think for a moment of the Great Commandment: "Hear, O Israel: The LORD our God, the LORD is one. Love the LORD your God with all your heart and with all your soul and with all your strength" (Deuteronomy 6:4-5, NIV). *Shema*, the word for "hear" in Hebrew, is one of the least understood words in Judaism. Rabbi Jonathan Sacks has pointed out that this word is almost "untranslatable into English since it means so many things: to hear, to listen, to pay attention, to understand, to internalise, to respond, to obey."[1] Repeatedly Moses told the people, "Shema." In other words, "*Hear* what God says. *Listen to* what God wants. *Pay attention to* the Divine Whisper. *Understand* what God desires. *Internalize* the words God speaks. Above all, *respond* to God and *obey* God's voice."

Notice as well that the command to listen precedes being told to love God with all our being. We cannot love someone well without first listening to them. Listening indicates our willingness to understand what the other person values, what they think, how they feel, what they like and dislike. As we grow in our understanding of who they are, we can express our love for them much more meaningfully. Listening, as it has often been said, is the first act of love. Similarly, when we listen to God, we can show our love for God more faithfully and purposefully by doing what God wants and values. Can you see how important listening to God is for us to discern God's personal will for our life?

Whenever we speak about listening to God, two questions often arise: How does God speak to us, and how do we go about listening? In the rest of this chapter, and the next one, I will share what I have been discovering as I have explored these questions. My discoveries have turned my friendship with God into much more of a two-way adventure. They have also helped me gain greater clarity about the shape of my personal calling in this season of my life. I hope that the same will happen for you.

## God Speaks in Scripture

Our touchstone for listening to God is Scripture. While God speaks in different ways—through the wonders of creation, conversations we have, books we read, sermons we listen to, dreams that come in the night, the heartbreak we suffer, the history of the church, the list goes on and on—our main listening post, where we hear God's word to us most reliably, is in the pages of the Bible. Long before Christ followers owned their own Bibles, they would come together and listen as passages were read aloud. They would listen not just to get information but to hear what God was saying to them. They knew that, if they were to be faithful to God's specific will for their lives, they needed to respond to God's voice in Scripture.

How do we develop this listening approach to the Bible? By keeping three things in mind:

1. *We believe that God speaks to us through Scripture.* The words in the Bible are not only inspired by the Holy Spirit but also the *means* through which God communicates with us here and now. This is the testimony of God's people throughout the centuries. When we read the Scriptures with a listening heart, we can expect the Living Author to meet us and address us personally. It is always appropriate, therefore, before we read our Bibles, to pray with Samuel, "Speak, LORD, for your servant is listening" (1 Samuel 3:9).

Believing that God speaks through Scripture does not mean we overlook its human side. The sixty-six biblical books were written over hundreds of years and against cultural and historical backgrounds radically different from ours. The human authors understood our world and the universe differently from the way we do with our modern technological and scientific viewpoint. The Bible also contains various kinds of writing, including history, poetry, songs, prophecy, parables, biography, law, and story. While these different genres call for deeper biblical study and honest inquiry above all, we must let God talk to us through the human authors.

2. *We distinguish between God and the Bible.* Bible scholar Scot McKnight explains that "God existed before the Bible existed; God exists independently of the Bible now. God is a person; the Bible is paper."[2] Distinguishing between the Person and the paper brings home the importance of listening to God as we read the Bible. Too often we can read the words of the Bible without paying attention to what God is saying to us. When I gave my daughter her first Bible, I wrote inside, "As you read these words on paper, may you listen to the Person behind the words."

Let me illustrate this distinction. When I leave for a ministry trip, Debbie often gives me a letter to read when I get to my destination. I will read that letter again and again. But there is a big difference between the paper and Debbie. The letter invites me into a deeper closeness, not with the words written on the paper but with the person behind the letter. When I have read the letter, I will phone her and say something like "I read your letter. Your words mean the world to me. Thank you for your love and for sharing it with me." Similarly, when we read the Bible, we are not interacting with paper. We are listening to the Living Author, who speaks to us through the words on the paper.

3. *We read the Bible with the attitude of someone who wants to learn to love God more deeply.* We want to meet God and do God's will. This means we come to Scripture humbly, with an open heart and mind. We put aside our own agenda and turn our attention to God's agenda for our lives. We cannot demand that God speak to us about whatever situation we are in. Rather, we ask God to share with us whatever is on God's heart for our lives. We are patient, and we wait. We are ready to hear what God wants to say, and we are willing to be obedient. We are not primarily looking for information; rather, when we open the Bible, we want to hear God's Divine Whisper so we can better discern how God wants us to live and what God wants us to do.

## Discernment Exercise

*Take time to read a favorite passage of Scripture. Practice the suggestions above about developing a listening approach to the Bible. Read your chosen passage with the expectancy that God wants to meet with you. Keep the distinction between Person and paper. Listen for God as you read the words on the page. Tell God your desire to hear whatever the Spirit wants to say.*

*Share with God your willingness to be obedient. Now listen and wait. Afterward, reflect on your experience of reading Scripture in this way. What are you learning? Write this down somewhere you can reference easily later.*

## Reading Scripture through the Lens of Jesus Christ

We listen to God in Scripture best when we read the Bible through the lens of Jesus Christ. Let me share a little of my journey in this regard. When I first read the Bible in my teenage years, it instantly got my attention. I had never read anything like this before. It pulsated with the "electricity" of God's presence and activity. On almost every page, I met the living God, who spoke and acted in the lives of ordinary human beings. As I read, my desire to get involved with this same God grew exponentially. I wanted to live with God in my own world, like the people I read about in the Bible lived with God in theirs.

I soon ran into some difficult questions, however. As I read those parts in the Bible, especially in the Old Testament, where God is portrayed as violent and aggressive—wiping out nations in anger, punishing enemies with plagues, justifying the rape of women—I did not know how to respond. How was I meant to interpret these stories of genocide, murder, rape, and abuse? How was I supposed to respond to God in these passages of terror? What could God be saying to me through them? I knew that if the Bible is the benchmark of my listening to God, I had to find a way of reading these biblical passages that would lead me into a deeper love for God rather than filling me with revulsion and outrage toward a violent God who would command such things to happen.

I found this way in Jesus Christ. The opening chapter of the book of Hebrews helped me a great deal: "In the past God spoke to our ancestors through the prophets at many times and in various ways, but in these last days he has spoken to us by his Son, whom he appointed heir of all things, and through whom also he made the universe. The Son is the radiance of God's glory and the exact representation of his being, sustaining all things by his powerful word" (verses 1-3, NIV).

Here we learn that Jesus is the supreme and definitive representation of who God is. If we want to tune in to God speaking to us through the Scriptures, whatever we hear needs to be in harmony with what we know of God through Jesus. He perfectly embodies God's true character, nature, and heart toward us. As Archbishop Michael Ramsey once wrote so beautifully, "God is Christlike and in him is no un-Christlikeness at all."[3]

Since God is Christlike, the best way to get to know God is to keep company with Jesus. We do this by reading the Gospels. We need to go through them repeatedly, one paragraph at a time, slowly and reflectively. When we look at God through the lens of Jesus' words and life, his death and resurrection, we come to know God personally—and to know what God is really like. We come to see that, as the sun always shines, God's compassion constantly flows toward us. We learn from Jesus that God *is* Love (1 John 4:8). God *cannot* stop loving the world or stop loving you and me.

When we know that God is love, and that we are unconditionally and personally loved by God, we position ourselves to better discern God's word in difficult biblical passages. God is not going to ask or say anything that will be unloving or un-Christlike. Should God be portrayed as saying or doing anything seemingly inconsistent with the self-sacrificing love of Jesus, we may need to spend more time wrestling with the text. The passage we are reading may reflect a picture of God that needs to be reframed in the blazing light of Jesus' gospel life.

For example, you may read one of the Old Testament stories where God commands the Israelites to kill their enemies.

While we certainly do not dismiss this passage or pretend it is not in Scripture, we read it with an awareness that it represents a developing and unfolding understanding of who God is. We must bring our listening for God's word in these difficult passages into conversation with our knowledge of Jesus. He reveals fully a God of amazing grace who loves every human being and who wants us to do the same.

Living in the tension brought about by difficult passages where God seems to act violently or condone violence is not easy. But until we can talk face-to-face with God about these things in the future, we need to stay close to Jesus right now as we read these portrayals of a God of violence and war. Over the years, as I have learned how to read the Bible through the lens of Jesus' life, death, and resurrection, these difficult passages have become the most important places where God speaks to me—especially when they are viewed in the light of the One who said, "You have heard that it was said . . . But I say to you . . ." (Matthew 5:21-22). Indeed, learning to see God through the gospel lens that Jesus Christ provides has become the measuring rod by which I assess all my other listening encounters with God.

Here is a simple way of reading a difficult biblical passage through the eyes of Jesus. We imagine ourselves sitting with Jesus, listening to him read the words to us. We know that, as the living Word, he is fully present. We acknowledge him to be the key to discerning God's word in the Bible. We share with him our wish to hear his heavenly Father speak to us. We raise with him the questions we have about the text. We keep our focus on him and let him reveal the meaning of the passage. We stay alert for any words, phrases, or ideas from the passage that may draw us deeper into Abba Father's unconditional love. We let Christ, who dwells in our heart, be our Living Teacher.

---
### Discernment Exercise
---

*Imagine sitting with Jesus and listening to him read Scripture to you.
There is a story at the beginning of Luke's Gospel where Jesus is
reading the Scriptures to the people (Luke 4:16-21). The passage Jesus
reads comes from Isaiah chapter 61. Look at the passage in the Old
Testament and notice what sentences Jesus leaves out when he quotes
it for the congregation. As you listen to Jesus read this passage to you,
be alert for whatever word, phrase, or sentence catches your attention.
How does this passage resonate with your life and situation right now?
Share with Jesus the thoughts and feelings that his words stir in you,
and listen to what he may be saying to you.*

---

## Praying the Scriptures

We listen to God through Scripture when we pray the Scriptures.
In the early years of following Christ, my praying was separate
from my Bible reading. I would talk to God, and when I had finished talking, I would open my Bible and read a passage. This way
of reading Scripture would focus mainly on getting more insights
and information that I could then apply to my life. Looking back
now, I can see that the listening part of prayer was neglected.
During these "quiet times," as they were called then, I seldom had
any sense that God was speaking to me. I still needed to learn how
to listen to God.

My lightbulb moment came on my first retreat, which was
in 1978. I remember it clearly. In a time of spiritual emptiness,
I knocked on the door of a retreat center called Koinonia in Bez
Valley, Johannesburg. Sister Liz, a Dominican nun wearing blue
jeans, a chunky sweater, and sneakers, welcomed me. She took me

to a small room sparsely furnished with a bed, table, chair, crucifix, open cupboard, and three coat hangers.

She suggested that I spend time with the words of Jesus in John 7:37-39, where he speaks about our need for those streams of living water that his Spirit alone can give. Anytime I wanted to chat, she said, we could arrange a time.

After hanging up my clothes, I sat down on the side of the bed, opened my Bible, and read the three verses. I thought about them for a while, and then, about thirty minutes later, went downstairs to find Sister Liz and to ask her for another biblical passage. She smiled and suggested that I stay with these verses a bit longer. You may not believe this, but she encouraged me to stay with those three verses for the whole three days! During that time, I gradually learned what it meant to bring my praying and Bible reading together into one action. I discovered what it meant to "pray the Scriptures." Reading the Bible became the means through which I listened to the Lord and spoke with him.

Let me try to describe what happened within me as I prayed the Scriptures on that retreat. In my desperate thirst, I felt myself drawn to the Living Water. I had the sense of the risen Jesus speaking to me personally, inviting me to come to him, and touching my heart through the words on paper. As his words went on that long journey from my lips and ears to my mind and then into my heart, I savored them, reflected on them, and carried them around with me. And as I wondered what they might mean for me, I knew that Christ was meeting me in them. From a deep place in my heart, an intense longing was born that found expression in a simple request: *Lord, please pour your living water into my thirsty soul.*

Over forty years have passed since that experience of praying the Scriptures. Today the journey continues. Almost every morning, I sit quietly with a passage of Scripture, read it aloud slowly, listen for a word from the Lord, respond to it, and take it with me into the day. Sometimes I use the same Scripture passage for a few days—or a week, a month, or maybe even longer. While I am reluctant to reduce this way of listening to God into a regimented spiritual technique, let me outline below what I like to call the five *P*s of praying the Scriptures. Even though they are a mixture of nouns and verbs, I hope they encourage you to give this way of listening to the Lord in Scripture a try.

## Becoming a Shema Person

As we read the Scriptures with a listening heart, we will begin to get a clearer sense of God's general will and personal will. We will see how God wants us to love our neighbor, walk in the light, serve those in need, and work for justice. These general guidelines (along with many others) express what God wants for all of us. They provide you and me with a broad moral imagination in which we can live faithfully as God's friends in God's world. More than this, as we listen to God in the Bible, we will also sense God calling us by name, speaking to us with startling clarity and immediate relevance. In moments like these, we experience God leading and guiding us into our personal calling for our lives. Let us therefore become a Shema people in a talkative world!

## Discernment Exercise

*These are the Five Ps of praying the Scriptures.*

Place. *Find a place where you can be alone and uninterrupted. Jesus said, "When you pray, go into your room and shut the door" (Matthew 6:6, ESV). Set aside a time to go to this listening post regularly.*

Prepare. *Begin your prayer by taking time to settle down in the silence. Do whatever helps you become quieter within yourself. Maybe you will take a few deep breaths, or repeat your favorite verse of Scripture, or look at a burning candle as a symbol of the light of Christ. Consciously acknowledge God's presence around you and within you. Ask for the help of the Holy Spirit to hear whatever God may want to say to you. Look at God looking at you through the divine gaze of unconditional love. Do not rush this time of preparation.*

Passage. *Read your chosen passage of Scripture aloud slowly, as the psalmist often encourages us to do. You may want to imagine the risen Jesus with you, reading the words to you. Hear the words first with your ears and then with your mind. Listen carefully for a word, phrase, or sentence that seems to speak to you or connect with your experience. If nothing seems to resonate, choose a word, phrase, or sentence that you would like to dwell on. Above all, do not be in a hurry with this reading. If we want to develop a listening approach to Scripture, we must not speed-read!*

Ponder. *When you have your word, phrase, or sentence, stop reading and begin meditating on Scripture. Open your mind and heart to receive the word, phrase, or sentence, and let it sink into your inner depths. Personalize the word as if it is spoken directly to you, internalize it, reflect on its meaning for your life, and absorb it inwardly, letting the Spirit bring it alive within you. All the time seek to listen to God with "the ears of your heart" to tune in to what God may be saying to you.*

Pray. *When this session's absorbing of God's Word seems complete, talk with the Lord about your response to what he has said to you. Share from your heart, freely and simply, how his Word has touched you. Tell the Lord what his Word means for you and how it affects your personal circumstances. Usually this phase of talking with the Lord will eventually bring you into a quieter space in which you can sit in silence and surrender yourself again to the Lord. Or it may lead you into a time of praise and worship in which you commit yourself to a specific act of obedience.*

*Over the next few days, you may like to try praying the Scriptures with these three passages: Isaiah 43:1-4; Matthew 11:29-30; and John 7:37-39. (At the back of this book, you will find a one-year outline of biblical passages that will take you through the four Gospels and the book of Acts. See appendix 2.)*

Chapter 5

# ATTENDING TO THE MOVEMENTS OF OUR HEART

*Discernment of spirits is the development of a deepening
moment-by-moment awareness of where our thoughts, feelings,
desires, and moods are coming from and leading to.*

ANNEMARIE PAULIN-CAMPBELL

The Bible is not the only place where God meets us and speaks to us. Earlier we explored the good news that God is always present and active throughout our world. Wherever we are, and whatever we are doing, God is there. God constantly communicates with us in all our experiences: through creation around us, our encounters with others, the crises and challenges we face, the heartaches and heartbreaks we go through, our daily work and tasks, as well as the big events taking place throughout the world. While we always begin with Scripture, we also need to recognize how God's communications come to us in the rest of our everyday lives.

This raises another set of questions. How do we know when God is communicating with us? How do we distinguish between those experiences in which God is present and speaking to us and those when God is not? How do we know what is "of God" and what is "not of God"? These questions must be explored if we are to cultivate a discerning heart.

As we have already noted, discernment involves recognizing God's active presence and voice so we can respond to what God is doing and saying and bring our lives more into harmony with God's dream for our world. This can only happen when we are aware of how and where God is calling us in our daily experiences and events.

A familiar story in the Bible sheds light on these questions. On the third day after the Crucifixion, two of Jesus' disciples were walking home from Jerusalem to Emmaus. Their hearts and hopes had been shattered by his death. As they walked along the road, a stranger (the risen Jesus) joined them and asked what they were talking about. They shared what had happened on that terrible Friday. The stranger interrupted their conversation and explained how the Scriptures say the Messiah would have to suffer. When they arrived at a fork in the road, the two pilgrims invited the stranger into their home.

As the three sat around the table and shared a meal together, the stranger suddenly took over the role of the host: He reached out for the bread, broke it, and gave each of them a piece. In that moment, they recognized him. It was Jesus, the One who had loved them so deeply and had given them hope. Then he vanished from their sight. "They said to each other, 'Were not our hearts burning within us while he was talking to us on the road, while he was opening the scriptures to us?'" (Luke 24:32). They got up and decided to return to Jerusalem to tell the other disciples what had happened.

Here is what I find significant: The hearts of the two disciples were burning within them when the stranger spoke to them on the road. They did not recognize what this burning meant, however, until Jesus broke the bread and gave it to them. The implications for our own lives are striking. There are many moments when God's presence and voice cause our hearts to burn but we fail to notice it. Sometimes it is only afterward, usually in a time of prayerful reflection, that we look back and notice the effects of the Spirit's activity within us. Sadly, we sometimes even miss God speaking by not paying attention to the movements of our heart.

Let us take a closer look at what "attending to the movements of our heart" involves.

## Our Inner Landscape

In our day-to-day lives, we experience a constant stream of insights, feelings, desires, emotions, intuitions, and moods. We could call this "the inner landscape" of our lives. Those Emmaus disciples remind us that whenever the Spirit of Christ moves within us, our inner landscape gets affected. Go back for a moment to the Emmaus road. There were two movements of the disciples' hearts. At first, as they walked along, they were feeling hopeless, disillusioned, and downcast. Then, when they encountered the risen Jesus, their inner thoughts and feelings changed even though they did not recognize this change at first. When they did, they said, "Were not our hearts burning within us while he was talking to us on the road?"

Two helpful terms describe these contrasting movements of the heart. They are *spiritual desolation* and *spiritual consolation*. I first came across these terms when I did the Spiritual Exercises of Ignatius in 1990.[1] The Exercises are a series of carefully structured,

Christ-centered meditations aimed at helping us discover a greater freedom in our walk with God. One of Ignatius's most valued contributions to Christ followers through the ages has been his teaching on what he termed "the discernment of spirits."

By this he meant paying attention to those inner movements of the heart that lead us *toward* God and those that pull us *away from* God. The first he called "spiritual consolation," and the second "spiritual desolation."

Ignatius's reasoning was straightforward. The Spirit of God always seeks to strengthen our faith, increase our hope, and grow our love for God and others. The Holy Spirit does this by prompting movements of "spiritual consolation" that draw us in a Godward direction. When we become aware of these God-prompted stirrings, they make us want to respond in faith and obedience. By contrast, "the enemy of our human nature," as Ignatius called the evil one, prompts the opposite movements of "spiritual desolation": feelings that draw us away from God. We should not allow ourselves to be led by these emotions, for they are not initiated by God's Spirit. As we will see later, spiritual desolation needs to be recognized when it occurs, and we need to learn how to deal with it creatively.

I found this insight enlightening. When it comes to our relationship with Christ, many of us believe that our thoughts are more important than our emotions. This view can be unhelpful. Not only do we develop a split spirituality between our mind and our heart, but we can end up with a faith that is purely rational and leaves our emotional lives untouched by the transforming love of God. While thoughts are critically important, so are feelings and emotions. They can become wonderful signals that point us to the leading of God's Spirit in our lives. This is the discovery that the Emmaus road pilgrims made, and so must we.

────────── *Discernment Exercise* ──────────

*Take some time to be quiet on your own. Ask the Holy Spirit to be with you as you reflect for a few moments on your inner landscape. Have there been any recent moments of "spiritual consolation" when your heart burned with faith, and hope, and love? You may find it helpful to go back to this moment and think about it a bit more. How and when did it come about? Where was this moment of spiritual consolation leading you? How did you respond to it? How would you like to respond to it now? You may like to make a few notes about this time of reflection.*

## Recognizing Spiritual Consolation

One of the most helpful things we can do to discern how God may be calling us is to recognize our inner movements of spiritual consolation. To do this wisely, we need to know what we mean when we use this term. So let me expand the basic description that I gave above of spiritual consolation being an inner movement in our heart that moves us in a Godward direction. I trust that a fuller description will help you become more aware of what is happening in your own inner landscape and to recognize those consoling movements through which the Spirit could be leading you forward right now.

To begin with, it must be stressed that spiritual consolation is not just "feeling good" or "being happy." While it certainly is a positive feeling, it is much more. The fact that we may be having good feelings because circumstances have turned out well does not necessarily mean we are experiencing *spiritual* consolation. Rather, this term refers specifically to a spiritual state directed by the action of the Spirit and intended to lead us toward God's personal will for our life. Our good or happy feelings take on spiritual significance only when they move us toward God in greater gratitude and obedience. In fact, we can even experience spiritual consolation in painful moments of sadness and loss.

Here are three kinds of experiences linked closely with spiritual consolation:

1. *Experiences that make us feel inwardly alive.* God's personal calling will always bring us to this point. Jesus said, "I have come to bring life, and to bring life in all its fullness" (John 10:10, author's paraphrase). To be alive is to become more responsive to life and those around us, to the beauty and wonder of creation, to the miracle of our own lives, and most especially, to the presence and activity of God that permeates our whole world. Paying attention to these life-giving moments, in which we sense the Spirit breathing newness of life into us, can help us become aware of how God may be pointing us toward God's specific will for our lives.

2. *Experiences that bear the marks of the fruit of the Spirit.* Paul wrote, "The fruit of the Spirit is love, joy, peace" (Galatians 5:22). Where these inner qualities of the Spirit are present, we can be reasonably sure that God is at work. Through our inner stirrings of love, God leads us into deeds of mercy and kindness; through our moments of joy, God reveals to us what we need for our well-being; through our profound sense of peace, God sheds light on our next step along the way toward faithfulness and purpose. When we experience this kind of movement within our hearts, it is highly likely that God is moving us in the direction of our personal calling from God.

3. *Experiences of sorrow for sin.* God often draws our attention to those bondages and blockages that sabotage our spiritual growth. When the Spirit is involved in this awareness of sin, we find that we are at the same time drawn more deeply into the consoling experience of God's love and mercy. The relief we feel is similar to what we sometimes experience when our doctor diagnoses what is wrong with us so that treatment can begin. By contrast, we can be sure that when we become negatively self-accusing and self-condemning about our sinfulness, we are experiencing spiritual desolation. In a nutshell, our rule of thumb for discernment is that *the chief way God leads and guides us is through spiritual consolation.*

Right now, I am seeking to discern how to live my present season of life faithfully and purposefully. Getting older brings diminishments of all sorts, yet I believe deeply that God's personal will relates to every season of our lives. During this time of discernment, I have found it immensely helpful to pay attention to those experiences of my work that bring me the greatest spiritual consolation. Two experiences stand out: giving the Spiritual Exercises of Ignatius and teaching on Zoom in the areas of spiritual formation and spiritual accompaniment.

As I have reflected on these consoling experiences, I have had the sense that through them the Spirit is saying to me, *Trevor, my personal calling in this current season of your life involves stepping away from the more public dimensions of your ministry into the more hidden ministries of leading others through the Spiritual Exercises and participating in online learning spaces where others want to grow in their faith and in the ministry of accompanying others on their spiritual journeys.*

--- *Discernment Exercise* ---

*You may like to try the reflective exercise that I have just described. Find a quiet space where you will not be interrupted. Ask the Holy Spirit to be with you as you enter this time of reflection. Recall three recent experiences in which you have felt spiritual consolation. These would be those experiences that gave you life or were characterized by the strong presence of the fruit of the Spirit or that led you along the road toward a renewed openness to God's merciful love. When you have finished describing them, look over them to notice any patterns, seeking to discern what God may be saying to you through them.*

## Dealing with Spiritual Desolation

The inner movements of spiritual desolation operate in the opposite way from those of spiritual consolation. These counter-movements refer to those times when we experience inner turmoil or a sense of lukewarmness in our faith or a distaste for the things of God. This may appear in different guises: confusion, discouragement, pessimism, self-preoccupation, hopelessness, despair, heaviness of spirit . . . and the list of negative signs goes on. While these experiences of desolation do not come from God, they certainly happen for us as we seek to discern God's personal will for our life.

The most important thing about spiritual desolation, Ignatius advised, was not to make any big decisions about our life direction during this time, especially ones that go back on decisions that we made in a time of spiritual consolation. The reason is obvious. Unlike movements of spiritual consolation, prompted by the Spirit of God, spiritual desolation comes from "the enemy of our human nature." Therefore, it would be far safer for us to identify when the desolation began, and what the reasons for it happening may be, rather than allowing it to push us into making decisions. Otherwise, we could make the mistake of allowing ourselves to be directed by that which has not come from God.

I have found this counsel hugely helpful. In my midtwenties I had the sense that God was calling me into the pastoral ministry. Since then, there have been two occasions when I have seriously questioned this call, wondering whether God was calling me elsewhere or whether I had mistaken God's personal will for my life. Both these times of questioning happened in times of spiritual desolation. Thankfully, wise friends encouraged me not to make life-changing decisions until I had dealt with the desolation and passed through it. They helped me see that God would guide me to understand my personal calling through my times of spiritual consolation and not through times of spiritual desolation.

There are many possible reasons for spiritual desolation. We may have neglected to care for our soul and lost our sense of connection with God. We may have come through a dark time, like being laid off, getting a divorce, or losing a loved one suddenly, which caused us to feel that we have been forgotten by God. We may be weary from overwork and have failed to care for ourselves properly. One frequent cause is in our relationships with others, especially where there is much resentment, anger, and hurt. All these experiences, and there are others, become possible openings for the evil spirit to prompt a movement away from God.

So what do we do when we are going through a time of spiritual desolation? Here are some practical tips: Be open about it with someone you trust, and ask the Lord for the light to see why it is happening now. Examine the different possible causes. Accept that it is a normal and necessary part of growing in a friendship with God. Talk with the Lord about it, and listen to what the Spirit may be saying to you. Keep your focus on God, even if you have lost your felt sense of God's presence. Remember that you are unconditionally loved by God in Christ and that spiritual consolation will return. Ask the Spirit to be your Teacher through this dark time. Consider the question *How is my desolation nudging me toward a more creative and life-giving way of living out my faith?* When we resist the temptations of spiritual desolation, we often find ourselves experiencing more spiritual growth than we would in moments of spiritual consolation.

Before ending this section, it may be helpful to say a little more about the temptations of spiritual desolation. At the top of the list would be the temptation to cooperate with that inner movement away from God. This may look different for different people. We may choose to give up on our times of praying the Scriptures. We may distance ourselves from friends who encourage us in our discipleship. We may believe that dark voice that tries to convince us of our unacceptability to God. We may give in to our sense of discouragement about our life and relationships. We may go along with the downward pull toward an activity that weakens our faith. We may become self-rejecting and self-condemning when faced with our sinfulness. Or, as already mentioned, we may go back on a decision that we made in an earlier time of spiritual consolation. In contrast, we can resist this temptation when we recognize spiritual desolation for what it is, turn toward God again in a posture of surrender, and ask for the grace to make a better choice that will be more in tune with what God wants for us right now.

---

### Discernment Exercise

*Think back to a recent time of spiritual desolation in your own life. (If you are in such a time right now, reflect on your present experience.) What were/are the signs of spiritual desolation? What do you think brought about this desolation?*

*Are you tempted to change any decision that you made in a time of spiritual consolation? How are you tempted to cooperate with this spiritual desolation? Which of the tips given on the previous pages connect helpfully with your experience? Make some notes of your reflections.*

---

## Learning to Notice

While God speaks to us primarily through Scripture, God also communicates with us through our personal experience. The Spirit of God is always present and active in your life and mine. When we take the time to attend to our inner landscape—and learn to notice those contrasting inner movements of spiritual consolation and spiritual desolation—we get clues about how God is leading and guiding us into our personal calling. Discernment involves both listening to God in Scripture and noticing how the Spirit is moving in our life so we bring our lives more in tune with what God wants for us. This is how we discover a life of greater faithfulness and purpose.

*Chapter 6*

# UNCOVERING AND
# EXERCISING OUR GIFTS

*When we talk about being true to ourselves—being the*
*persons we are intended to be—we are talking about gifts.*
*We cannot be ourselves unless we are true to our gifts.*

ELIZABETH O'CONNOR

There is a delightful story about Michelangelo, who once pushed a massive block of marble down a street. His neighbor sat lazily in front of his house and watched him with much curiosity. Wondering why Michelangelo struggled with this rough piece of stone, he asked why he was sweating away at what seemed a senseless task. Michelangelo is reported to have answered, "Because there is an angel in this rock that is longing to be released."

This story illustrates an important and exciting aspect of our faith. On the one hand, it reminds us that there is something wonderful within each one of us that God wants to bring forth. When Christ enters our lives, he takes the raw material of our lives that we offer him and makes something of it that is unlike anyone or anything else. He releases those strengths, capacities, and abilities that have been imprisoned. As a young Christ follower, I loved to sing the words of the chorus to "Something Beautiful," which was a constant reminder that as we offer Christ all our brokenness and strife, he makes something beautiful of our life.[1] As we yield ourselves to God, we are set free to become the person we are meant to be.

On the other hand, this story reminds us that God's personal will is written into the very fabric of our being. So often, we ask God to show us our calling without realizing that it is inscribed into how we have been made. After all, we are God's handiwork! We glimpse our specific vocation as we pay attention to those unique gifts we bring into the world. These gifts have been entrusted to us and, as we shall see, we will be held accountable for how we use them. Every person has the task of uncovering and exercising the gifts that have been placed within them. As we engage this creative task, we can be sure that God's Spirit will set free the angel hidden in the rock of our life.

Wonderfully, as we begin to use our gifts, we come alive. Whenever I find myself with someone struggling with a sense of meaninglessness, I wonder whether they have given time and effort to identifying and exercising their unique giftedness. We cannot become the person God wants us to be unless we are true to these gifts tucked away within us. Tragically, many of us go through our lives without ever allowing the Spirit of God to release what is most beautiful and good about us. Could it be that one of the most important ministries of the church is to be a community in which we help each other uncover and exercise our unique giftedness?

## A Gospel Parable about Gifts

Whenever this picture of the angel hidden within the rock comes to mind, I think of one of Jesus' parables. You may have guessed which one. It is the parable of the talents. Here is the gist of it. A wealthy landowner went on a long journey. Before he left, he took some of his capital profits and gave them to three of his servants to use on his behalf. To one he gave five talents, to the second two, and to the third just one. The first servant took his five talents and made another five. The second servant also doubled his two talents. Seemingly, they had appreciated what they had been given and trusted their master. The last servant, however, simply hid his talent in the ground, which was the equivalent of a safe-deposit box in the ancient world.

When the master returned, he praised the first two servants and gave them even greater responsibilities.

He said to each of them, "Well done, good and faithful servant! You have been faithful with a few things; I will put you in charge of many things. Come and share your master's happiness!" (Matthew 25:21, 23, NIV). However, when the third servant told him that he had been too scared to put his one talent to use and had hidden it in the ground, the master got upset with him. He took his one talent, gave it to the one who had ten, and said, "To all those who have, more will be given, and they will have an abundance; but from those who have nothing, even what they have will be taken away" (Matthew 25:29).

What are we to make of this? At first glance, the master seems unfair. Yet we know that the God we meet in Jesus Christ would never treat anyone unjustly. So here is my understanding of this parable. Each of us has been uniquely and differently gifted by our Creator. While the talents in the parable certainly have an economic reference, they also have a wider meaning. They represent the divine investment that God has made in us in terms of the abilities, competencies, and gifts that God has given us. What matters most is not how many talents we have, for there is little we can do about that. What really matters, and this for me is the central thrust of the parable, is what we do with what we have been given.

Jesus made it clear that God wants us to develop our talents and put them to good use. When we do, our lives grow, and we experience the joy of being creative and faithful servants. However, when we play it safe and bury our gifts, we know the feelings of deadness that usually accompany the unlived life. Like the one-talent person who hides their gift, we, too, experience "the outer darkness, where there will be weeping and gnashing of teeth" (Matthew 25:30). This is the sad consequence of not uncovering and exercising the talents that we have been given. Clearly, identification of our gifts, and their use in freedom and joy, lies at the heart of discerning God's personal will for our lives.

### Discernment Exercise

*When it comes to uncovering and exercising your abilities and talents, are you an undertaker (someone who buries their gifts), a caretaker (someone who plays it safe with their gifts), or a risk-taker (someone who trusts God enough to use their gifts adventurously)? Take some time to reflect on this question in as much detail as you can. What are your specific gifts? Should you struggle with identifying your specific gifts, picture yourself doing what you love to do and name the gifts that you use in this activity. Talk with God about these gifts and listen to what God may be saying to you about them.*

The question that faces us now is *How do we go about this adventure of uncovering and exercising our gifts?* Here are three thoughts to explore: affirming our unique giftedness, naming our unique giftedness, and exercising our unique giftedness.

## Affirming Our Unique Giftedness

The adventure begins as we affirm our unique giftedness.

Sometimes this can be a real struggle, especially for those of us who consider ourselves rather average human beings. Often, we feel that we do not bring anything remarkable into the world. Then, like the servant in the story, we go and hide whatever small talent we may have and think, *What difference can I really make? I do not have much ability. I cannot make a big contribution. What is the use of even trying? There is certainly no angel within me waiting to be released.* We may compare ourselves with the more obviously gifted and then blame God because we do not have better or more abilities. Or, like the third servant, we may excuse our lack of creativity by saying, "I was afraid. I did not have the courage to use the one talent that I was given. I thought God would be angry if I failed."

When we make excuses like these, we run from our unique giftedness. Consequently, God's personal calling in our lives gets frustrated and sabotaged. Remember what we emphasized earlier: God's specific will has been written into the very fabric of our beings through the gifts that have been planted in us. The message that God wants us to deliver, the song that God wants us to sing, the special act of love that God wants us to bestow—all these are bound up in some specific way with the talents invested in us by God. The denial of our talents and abilities, as we can see, has far-reaching consequences. To put it bluntly, if we do not use our gifts, we do not become who God wants us to be, and we do not do what God wants us to do.

Rather than avoiding our unique giftedness, we can affirm it. We do this when we say to ourselves something as simple as this: *I know that God has created me and given me life. My life, small as it may be, is valuable and worth more to God than I can ever imagine. Even though I may not be extremely gifted, I know that I bring something into this world that no one else brings. I also know that, if I offer to God whatever talent I have been given and develop it to its full potential, God will make something beautiful of my life. The angel within the rock of my life will be set free.* When we say yes to ourselves and to God and affirm our uniqueness, we discover that we can live fully with whatever gifts we have, provided we acknowledge and use what God has placed in us. Even more importantly, we begin to discover the joy of fulfilling God's personal will for our lives.

---

### Discernment Exercise

*Take some time to affirm your own unique giftedness. Perhaps you can do this by saying slowly and aloud the italicized sentences above. What feelings and thoughts do you have as you say yes to the way that God has created you? Share them with God, and pay attention to how you sense God responding to you.*

---

## Naming Our Unique Giftedness

The adventure continues as we name our unique giftedness.

While this is not always easy, it is vitally important. If we do not identify our gifts, they remain unwrapped and unused. We have already noticed the sad consequences when this happens. We miss out on the life that God longs for us to have. Another consequence, not yet mentioned, is that when they are not named, they seldom get developed. Naming our gifts usually brings the challenge of their long-term development and being put into practice. Some may feel apprehensive about the sacrifices this could involve, especially regarding time, energy, and finances. When we do name *and* nurture our gifts, however, we step into the life that God intends for each of us.

Sometimes we need affirmation from others to help us identify our giftedness. This happened for me. In my early twenties, I took part in a three-month leadership training program. One day we were asked in small groups to think about one another's lives and say what we valued about each person. The exercise started well. Each person in the group took a turn to listen while the rest of us affirmed what we appreciated about them. When my turn came, for what seemed a long time, the group was silent. I wondered what they were going to say. Finally, someone broke the silence and said, "Trevor, I think you can listen quite well."

To be honest, I was a bit disappointed at first. Listening just did not seem to be that great a gift. But I do remember offering that gift to God and committing myself to its development. Looking back now, I am deeply grateful for the opportunities God has given me to put this talent to use. Learning to listen carefully has taken me again and again into that sacred space that we call the "heart" of another person.

My understanding of what it means to be human in this world has been considerably deepened through listening. Somehow, being able to identify my gift has given my life tremendous meaning and purpose that I believe only comes from embracing God's personal will for our lives.

I share this personal experience only because it is ordinary and unspectacular. My hunch is that your talents might involve much more than "listening quite well"! I hope that the following discernment exercise will help you become even more aware of your own unique giftedness than you are right now. We will discover that our gifts often connect with things we enjoy doing, tasks we seem to do well, and personal qualities others appreciate.

Since talents normally find expression in action, I offer you the following list of gift areas to aid you in your thinking. Obviously, it is impossible to provide a comprehensive list of all possible gifts. Please feel free to add to this list or perhaps blend two or three actions that reflect your own gift mix.

---

### Discernment Exercise

*Take time to read through this list of gift areas and underline those activities that you enjoy, that you do well, or that others appreciate about you. This may facilitate the naming of your unique giftedness.*

| | | | |
|---|---|---|---|
| accounting | carpentry | flower arranging | plumbing |
| acting | clowning | gardening | praying |
| administering | coaching | giving | preaching |
| advising | computing | group facilitating | problem-solving |
| advocating | cooking | guiding | reading |
| affirming | counseling | helping | recording |
| analyzing | creating | interviewing | recruiting |
| arbitrating | critical thinking | knitting | relating |
| arranging | dancing | lecturing | researching |
| assessing | decorating | letter writing | sculpting |
| auditing | designing | listening | selling |
| baking | drawing | managing | sewing |
| banking | driving | marketing | singing |
| banner making | editing | motivating | speaking |
| bridge building | encouraging | nursing | supervising |
| budgeting | entertaining | organizing | teaching |
| building | filing | painting | team building |
| calculating | financing | photography | visiting |
| caring | fixing | piano playing | writing |

*How would you describe your own unique giftedness? How can you develop it more fully?*

---

## Exercising Our Unique Giftedness

Finally, our adventure involves the actual exercising of our unique giftedness in the service of others.

We must not keep the reflections from the previous exercise purely theoretical. We need to step out in faith and risk using the talents we have. There is an intimate connection between our gifts and how God wants us to serve in this world. Indeed, we often come to understand how we can best serve God by identifying *and* exercising our gifts. Sometimes we are reluctant to take this practical step. Just as we make excuses not to acknowledge our unique giftedness, when it comes to putting our talents to use, we again make more excuses. Could it be that we already possess, even if in undeveloped form, the gifts we need to make God's dream real in the world?

You may remember the story of the burning bush when God called Moses to free the Hebrews from their oppression. Before Moses said yes, he tried to sidestep his personal calling with a list of various excuses. They sound a lot like those we sometimes make when we sense God calling us to do something. Here's my loosely paraphrased version of his excuses: "I'm nobody." "I don't know enough about God." "What happens if I fail?" "I don't have what it takes." "Someone else can do it better."

Amid these excuses, God asked Moses, "What do you have in your hand?" (Exodus 4:2, author's paraphrase). It was an affirming question to help Moses recognize that he already possessed what he needed to step into God's calling for his life. At that moment Moses was holding a staff. God wanted to use this simple stick to begin the work of liberation for a nation.

When we, too, can bring our unique giftedness and risk exercising it on God's behalf, God's personal calling in our lives has a chance to be expressed. When we make available to God whatever we are holding in our hands and begin to use that talent in the service of those around us, we will be astonished with what God can do with it to make this world a better place.

Let me stress that I am not suggesting that we simply go ahead and exercise our talents without thought or reflection. Discernment is always necessary. We need to think carefully about the situation involved and how best our unique giftedness can be used in the service of those around us. Sometimes I find it helpful to ask two basic questions: *How can I use my talent to bless someone around me today?* and *How can I use my talent to give God a good reputation among my family, friends, colleagues, and neighbors today?* Once we have some clarity around these two questions, we can then go ahead and exercise the gifts entrusted to us, trusting that God will come alongside us and empower us for the work at hand.

Remember that God is interested in every aspect of human life. We have already emphasized that God is actively present in all things. Discernment involves bringing the whole of our life into harmony with God's ever-present activity, wherever we are and whatever we are doing. We do not serve God only with what are considered spiritual gifts, like prophecy and prayer. We also minister to others with natural abilities (like cooking, or administration, or repairing lawnmowers), especially when we put them to use on behalf of the well-being of the people around us. "Like good stewards of the manifold grace of God," the apostle Peter wrote, "serve one another with whatever gift each of you has received" (1 Peter 4:10).

If you are ready to risk exercising your giftedness to bless others, you may find the following discernment exercise a real adventure!

───────── *Discernment Exercise* ─────────

*Think of your own unique giftedness as you identified it in the last exercise. Now think of a specific way you could exercise your talent. You may want to talk about this with God, too. Consider an action that serves others in a practical and personal way. Ask the two questions suggested earlier in this section. Listen to God as you reflect on those questions. What activity or work comes to mind? Now step out and do something in the knowledge that God is with you as you put your gift to work.*

## Releasing the Angel Within

I hope that as you have read this chapter and engaged with the discernment exercises, you might have glimpsed the connection between discerning God's personal will and identifying your own unique giftedness. When we talk about becoming the person God wants us to be and doing what God wants us to do, we enter the inner world of our God-given talents.

An "angel" within each of us is waiting to be released. This work of liberation involves affirming that God has created us with specific talents, naming them and offering them to God, and then stepping out and using them for the well-being of others. When we set out on this adventure, we begin to discover the fullness of life that God intends for each of us.

*Chapter 7*

# REFLECTING ON OUR CIRCUMSTANCES

*With reflection comes insight and with insight the chance to
move forward in fresh directions with renewed hope.*

ANNE LONG

One simple sentence, from my first pastoral supervisor, has
significantly shaped how I seek to discern God's personal will.
Each Wednesday during my first year of congregational ministry, we met to review my pastoral activities over the past week.
One day I asked him why he always wanted me to reflect on
what had happened. I remember his answer clearly. Qualifying
a commonly held assumption, he replied, "Always remember,
Trevor, that we do not learn from experience; we learn when we
reflect on experience."

These words are important when it comes to discernment. We
have already seen that discerning God's personal will involves paying attention to those inward heart movements of consolation and

desolation. This happens as we reflect on our insights, feelings, emotions, desires, intuitions, moods, and our other responses. When we take the time to attend to this "inner landscape" and distinguish between those movements that lead us toward God and those that lead us away from God, we get clues about how God may be guiding us into our personal calling. Remember that God always leads us through experiences of spiritual consolation rather than those of spiritual desolation.

In this chapter I want us to go one step further. In our daily lives we also experience a wide variety of external circumstances. These involve encounters with people, challenges in our daily work, conversations we have, movies we watch, family conflicts we find ourselves in, curveballs that hit us, celebrations we enjoy, sports we watch, coincidences that surprise us, our different stages of life, and all the current events that happen in our day. The list is endless. If we want to identify how the Spirit may be leading and guiding us, we also need to examine this "outer landscape" of our lives.

## Our Mentor in the Reflective Life

Mary, the mother of Jesus, mentors us in the reflective life. Her example takes on added significance when we view it against the difficult circumstances she faced as a young mother. Think about them for a moment. She was heavily pregnant when she traveled over seventy miles with Joseph from Nazareth to Bethlehem. They struggled to find a safe place where she could give birth. They ended up in the messiness of a borrowed stable, where Jesus was born. After the visit of the wise men who brought gifts, she got the news about Herod's death squads coming to kill all boys under the age of two. This "outer landscape" gives us some idea of the upheaval going on in Mary's life when she took time to reflect.

Come with me now to the second chapter of Luke's Gospel. Hidden among these traumatic circumstances was one still moment. Without any fanfare or exaggeration, Luke records this reflective moment: "Mary treasured all these words and pondered them in her heart" (Luke 2:19). Later, in the same chapter, he records another reflective moment. This one took place amid the anxiety of the twelve-year-old Jesus going missing while his family was traveling back from Jerusalem. After this episode, we read, "His mother treasured all these things in her heart" (Luke 2:51). Twice in one Gospel chapter, Mary points us to the reflective life.

How do we picture these reflective moments in Mary's life? Most importantly, we must remember that Mary was Jewish. She belonged to a people who repeatedly remembered their history and reflected on it.

They did this knowing that they were involved with a God who was present and active, in both their personal and national histories. This was the standpoint of faith from which Mary reflected. We can imagine her mulling over these events and encounters in her life, again and again, asking questions like *God, where are you in these circumstances? What are you doing? What are you saying to me? How do you want me to respond? What does it mean to be your faithful servant? What is your personal will for my life?*

Will you let Mary mentor you in this practice of reflection? Her questions help us understand what we must ask as we seek God's personal will amid our own external circumstances. We can be sure that as we engage these questions reflectively, we will get hints of the Spirit's leading.

## The Spiritual Value of Reflection

Why is the practice of reflecting on our circumstances important? Remember, there is one central conviction on which discernment is based. Here it is again: *The Bible witnesses to God's active presence in every experience, every encounter, and every event.* There is no place in our everyday lives where God is absent. We must resist any kind of split spirituality that separates our lives into spiritual and nonspiritual compartments. The divine footprint is present in all our circumstances. God wants to meet us in all the realities of our daily lives. However, we will only discern how God is present and active in these things when we reflect on them.

This is how discernment works. We reflect on the outer landscape of our lives to catch glimpses of how God has been present and active in those events. While we often cannot see God coming, it is easier to look back and discern how God has been with us. Learning to recognize God's activity in our lives makes it possible for us to respond to God more faithfully as we go forward. It helps us purposefully align our own decisions and choices with God's action in and around us. By fine-tuning our antennae to "hear" God's voice speaking through our circumstances, we build the foundation for a life of faithful discipleship.

Here is a practical example I find helpful. Cars have a windshield and a rearview mirror. Both are necessary. We drive looking forward, but if we want to drive safely, we must look now and then in our rearview mirror. If we do not have this habit firmly in place, we will drive in a way that may cause an accident. However, we do not spend all our time looking backward. The front windshield gets our primary attention; notice that it is much bigger than the rearview mirror. Similarly, our journey along the road of discipleship with Christ requires a balance between looking forward and looking backward if it is to be faithful and wise.

Failing to take time to glance backward blocks our efforts to discern God's will going forward for our good. Think about what happens when we live without reflection. Without trying to gain insight into why we do certain things, we often make the same mistakes again, repeat destructive patterns of behavior, and fall into unhelpful ruts as we respond to our circumstances. We miss out on abundant living. Only when we reflect upon our experiences of success and failure and listen to what God may be saying to us can we discern how God may be leading us forward into those possibilities that will bring us more deeply into the fullness of life that God wants to give each of us—an ever-deepening shared life with God and those around us, a life of ongoing inner transformation into the loving image of Christ, a life characterized by the joy and peace of the Holy Spirit that is not determined by external circumstances, and a profound inner assurance that our dying is a passageway into the inexhaustible and immeasurable depths of God's love.

When we fail to reflect, we may also miss the hidden blessings that come our way. God's loving gifts get tucked away in our daily circumstances. Without reflection they may go unrecognized.

We may overlook the good things people have said to us, the things they've done that have blessed us, and those many unexpected moments that have brought meaning and joy into our lives. Carving out some space to reflect on these grace-permeated circumstances makes us more aware of the different ways God's love touches our lives and gives us clues as to how God wants us to pass this love on to others.

---
### Discernment Exercise
---

*Reflecting on our circumstances, in the faith that God is lovingly present in all things, leads us to pray with confidence and hope:*

*"Lord, thank you for your footprints in all the circumstances of my life, from the moment of my beginning until now. You have been lovingly present and active in everything that has happened, even in those painful things that you did not want to happen. Thank you for rejoicing with me in my joys and grieving with me in my losses. Right now, help me discern what you are saying to me in the events going on around me so that I can bring my life more in step with your dream for our world. I ask this with all the love and longing of my heart. Amen."*

## Making God's Dream Real

One way to discern God's personal will is to explore what it may mean for us to make God's dream more real in our unique external circumstances. Remember once again our description of discernment: *Discernment is learning to recognize God's active presence and to listen to God's voice so that we may bring our lives into harmony with what God wants for us and play our part in keeping God's big dream for the world alive.*

Discerning God's personal will for our lives is always connected with God's overall will for our world. In other words, God calls each of us by name to play our part in making this universe a more harmonious, friendly, and life-giving place for all, wherever we are. We find out what this might mean when we take the time to reflect on our present circumstances. Here is a glimpse of how we can go about this in three important areas of our outer landscape:

1. Reflecting on the state of our *personal relationships* is always a good place to start. The acid test of our relationship with God is the quality of our relationships with those around us. The apostle John put it bluntly: "Those who do not love a brother or sister whom they have seen, cannot love God whom they have not seen" (1 John 4:20). So we can ask: *Where is there unresolved conflict? Where is there a need for apology? Where does forgiveness need to be offered? Who in my family circle needs my time and attention?* Considering these questions prayerfully and listening for the Spirit's promptings of love in our hearts could shed light on the way we can make God's dream more real in our present relationships.

2. A key area of reflection is our *daily work*. Our most important mission trip is the one we take to work each day. This is where we, as followers of Christ, are called to make God's love more visible. While our daily work is how we provide a living for ourselves and our families, there is much more to it. It is one of the most important arenas where we are called to bring our lives into harmony with what God wants for the world. Whatever the nature of our work may be—retail, technical, medical, educational, legal—we need to discern what it means for us to love God and serve our neighbor in this challenging place.

3. Another area for reflection is *our engagement with the pain and suffering of our community.* Each one of us is called to bring God's love into contact with the brokenness that surrounds us. Obviously, we cannot address all the human need in our midst. We cannot visit all the shut-in elderly; care for all the destitute; get alongside all the sick, bereaved, and dying. We cannot minister to all those experiencing poverty, violence, or

unemployment. But we can ask God, *What human cry most disturbs me? Where do my gifts and abilities most connect with the need I come across? What is the little piece of God's dream that I am called to live out?* Reflecting on these questions could lead us to take our first small steps of love in making God's dream more real for those who suffer around us.

As we ponder three areas of our outer landscape, we can be sure that our reflection will spark many thoughts and feelings. It is not always easy to discern which of these we need to get involved with and act on. Here again we must pay attention to those inner movements of our heart. Reflective thoughts and feelings that are prompted by the Spirit will be marked by spiritual consolation. They will bring us alive, deepen our relationship with God, and be characterized by a settled peace. They will not leave us dead inside, separated from God, and agitated. Our guideline remains: The Lord leads us by way of consolation and not by desolation. Your personal calling, as Frederick Buechner once beautifully pointed out, "is the place where your deep gladness and the world's deep hunger meet."[1]

---

### Discernment Exercise

*Pick one of the three areas and reflect on it in your next time of prayer. As you keep in mind God's big dream for our world, ask the Spirit to show you what your little piece of that dream may look like. Bring your wonderings about what God may be doing and saying to you through your external circumstances into your prayer. Be aware of the inner movements of your heart throughout your time of reflection. Afterward, you may want to make some notes in your journal.*

---

## The Practice of Daily Reflection

The practice of daily reflection keeps us in tune with what God may be doing and saying in our daily lives. I was first introduced to a practice called the Examen when I did the Spiritual Exercises of Ignatius. Each night I was encouraged to look back over my day and ask for the Spirit's light as I reflected on what had taken place. This practice became the highlight of the whole Ignatian journey for me. While I have not always practiced it in its entirety, I still find some form of daily reflection at the end of each day hugely helpful in discerning God's personal will. Here are the five basic steps of the daily Examen:

1. *Ask for the help of the Spirit.* This time of reflection is not so much a thought exercise as it is a prayer exercise. We want to reflect with God. We want God to bring to our attention those things to which we need to attend. We want to talk with God about our lives and not just think them on our own. Above all, we want to recognize what God may be saying to us and doing in our lives so that we can bring our lives more into alignment with God's personal will.

2. *Notice the gifts or blessings you have received throughout the day.* These do not have to be big. Usually they include simple things like an early morning walk or run, the first cup of coffee, a greeting from a stranger, an encouraging phone call, the completion of a task, a walk in the garden, and so on. As we thank God for moments like these, the simple blessings we receive each day become powerful reminders of God's loving presence enfolding us. When we apply this practice of gratitude regularly, we will discover that our awareness of God's loving presence and activity gradually increases.

3. *Review the moods, thoughts, emotions, and feelings that you have experienced throughout the day.* This inner landscape usually fluctuates depending on what has taken place in the outer landscape of the day. So we begin this step by replaying the events of the day in our mind. Two questions are especially helpful as we do this: *When did I feel alive, energized, and responsive today?* and *When did I feel dead inside, drained, and apathetic today?* Asking ourselves simple questions like these help us reflect on those contrasting subtle heart movements of spiritual consolation and spiritual desolation that help tremendously in discerning how God may be guiding us. As one example, when I notice feelings of desolation about my marriage, I find it helpful to reflect on how I am relating to Debbie and then to allow my sense of heaviness to nudge me toward making choices in my marriage that are more loving, life-giving, and creative.

4. *Reflect on your failures to respond to God's love and to express it to others.* Rather than making this exercise one of feeling bad about ourselves, it is much more helpful to ask God to help us with this reflection. *Lord, please help me be aware of those attitudes and actions today that have been unloving and hurtful.* When *God* does this heart searching, instead of our own inner critic, the result will not be the desolation of self-accusation. Rather, as we confess the failures that God brings to our attention, our confession will lead us toward the consolation of an ever-deepening awareness of God's forgiveness and acceptance. If it leads us to wallow in guilt and shame, we have done this step wrong.

5. *Look forward to tomorrow, and ask for whatever help and guidance is needed to make God's dream more real in your life.* This

is often the most creative step in our reflection. We imagine what we will be doing in the day ahead, the challenges we will be facing, the people we will be seeing, the choices that will be facing us, and whatever else may be on the agenda. As we think about these coming possibilities, we ask God for what we will need to live creatively, wisely, and faithfully. Most especially, with an awareness of how we may have failed today, we ask for help in those specific areas where we might be tempted to drift away from God's will and Way.

I hope that this description of the Examen kindles your desire to practice it. Over the years I have learned that it can be done in different ways. Sometimes we may focus on just those one or two steps that seem especially relevant. At other times, we may put all the steps aside and simply sit with God and ask the Spirit to bring to our awareness from the past day whatever we need to look at more carefully. However we choose to follow the steps, this time of prayer should not take longer than ten minutes or so. It will sharpen our sensitivity to the nudges and promptings of the Spirit. It will keep us in tune with the presence and activity of God in the different aspects of our everyday lives. Above all, it will help us discern God's personal will.

## Discernment Exercise

*Set aside ten to fifteen minutes to prayerfully reflect—with the Lord— on the past twenty-four hours. For this first time, practice all five steps as they are outlined here. Afterward, write down a few words (not more than twenty or so) describing how it was for you.*

## Becoming a Reflective Person

I will always be grateful for those words spoken to me by my pastoral supervisor almost fifty years ago. His insight about reflecting on our experiences has helped me, more times than I can remember, to notice what God may be doing and saying in my life. God is constantly inviting us into a divine encounter within our ordinary, everyday moments. When we take the time to reflect on them, we discover for ourselves that God's presence and activity permeates every aspect of our lives. This discovery can lead us into the adventurous possibilities of discerning how God is calling us by name to realize God's dream right where we are.

*Chapter 8*

# ENGAGING IN SACRED CONVERSATIONS

> *To think of conversation as a sacred art challenges us to imagine all the conversations in which we participate, from the acquaintance we run into at Target to the dialogue for which we've spent weeks in preparation, as a potentially sacred conversation.*
>
> DIANE M. MILLIS

We seldom discern God's personal will all alone. The glimpses we get of our personal calling are enriched as we engage in conversations with others.

When we explore with others what God wants for us, we get surprising insights that give important clues as to how the Spirit wants to lead us. You may have experienced this. You might find yourself unclear about your next step in a certain situation, even after praying about it, and remain unclear about how to proceed. Then one day you talk things over with a caring friend, and the way ahead becomes clearer. Looking back on this encounter, you become aware that God used this conversation to guide you.

We should not be surprised by this. When we open our lives

to Christ, he always comes with his arms around his family. We do not follow him solely on our own. The Bible knows nothing of spirituality in isolation. We discern God's personal will as part of God's people. While we need time on our own with the Lord to prayerfully reflect on what is happening within and around us, we also need interaction with other Christ followers. The risen Christ promises to be with us through these conversations with our companions in the faith. Jesus said, "Where two or three are gathered in my name, there am I in the midst of them" (Matthew 18:20, RSV). As we share with one another, making room for his Spirit, who is always there with us, we open ourselves to God's leading and guidance.

There is another reason why discernment requires conversation. Our individual perception of the situations facing us is often extremely limited. Sometimes we are blind to our patterns of thinking and fail to see how God may be present and active in other ways within and around us. Undoubtedly, we need to dialogue with others to expand our view of what God may be doing and saying. We often interpret our experiences through lenses that blind us to a wider picture of what is going on spiritually. It may take a conversation with another faithful follower of Christ for us to see things more clearly. Often God reveals one part of the picture to one person and another part to someone else.

While God is present and active in all our interactions, we also need to set aside conversational space to reflect on what God may be saying and doing in our lives. These encounters are referred to in this chapter as *sacred conversations*.[1] They happen when we get together with someone we trust and whose faith journey we respect. They are grace gifts as we seek to discern God's personal will for our lives. Anyone wanting to go deeper in their discerning journey will have shared in several such conversations. Without these kinds of interactions along our spiritual journey, it is highly unlikely that we will grow in the adventure of discernment.

Let me try to describe how a sacred conversation can happen for you in your everyday life. Possibilities for such occasions are more present than we usually think. We can have these kinds of conversations with those closest to us: with colleagues at work, with our next-door neighbor, with someone in our small group, or with a stranger in a parking garage. They take place when three conditions are met: (1) we learn to listen well to each other, (2) we develop an ability to ask wondering questions, and (3) we risk sharing what is most real in our own lives. Let me explore each of these in turn with the hope that they will open for you a deeper engagement in sacred conversations with those around you. This could also lead you into clearer discernment of how God is present and active in your life right now.

---

### Discernment Exercise

*Recall a recent conversation that you would describe as "sacred." What made it sacred? In what way was it a gift of grace in your own discerning journey? Perhaps you have never had a conversation in which you have reflected on how God may be active and present in your life. Can you imagine what a sacred conversation could be like for you? Can you identify a potential spiritual friend with whom you could have such a conversation?*

---

## Learning to Listen Well

Sacred conversations involve listening well to each other. Or as James encouraged his readers: "Be slow to speak and quick to listen" (James 1:19, author's paraphrase).

Learning to listen well lies at the heart of a sacred conversation. This is a demanding and lifelong journey. How often do we hear comments like "You're not listening to me," "Let me finish my sentence," or "That is not what I am saying"? These typical responses underline the fact that there is a massive difference between merely hearing the words someone says and really listening to understand better what their words mean for them. If we cannot listen to each other well, it is nearly impossible for us to be able to listen well to the God who is constantly communicating with us through our experiences and encounters. When we are deaf to our neighbor, we become deaf to God, too.

How do we go about learning to listen well?

1. *Listening well involves talking less.* It can be hard for some of us to rein in our constant chatter. Our tongue seems to have a life of its own. On a recent retreat, one retreatant acknowledged that they were addicted to talking. We need to check whether this is true for us as well. Interestingly, James pointed out that if we cannot control our tongue, our religion is useless (James 1:26). Controlling our tongue is the first step toward listening to those around us. Furthermore, it is only when we begin to listen to others that we find ourselves able to listen to what God may be saying to us as well. It is almost impossible to listen to Someone we cannot see if we cannot listen to someone we do see!

   We must learn to be silent—however, not just with our lips. We also need to become quiet within ourselves. This requires a certain self-assurance. When we feel secure within, we can listen to others more freely, even when they say things that we see differently. It means that we will not become upset easily when the other person expresses views with which we strongly disagree. We simply listen with an open heart and mind to what is shared. I have often been struck by how God has spoken to me through something that initially disturbed me. If we close the conversation by getting into an argument, we could miss what the Spirit wants to say to us. The sacredness of our conversation gets lost.

2. *Listening well demands patience.* Sacred conversations seldom happen if we are rushed. We need time to reveal ourselves to each other, at our own pace and in our own time. Telling someone to "get to the point" often prevents them from disclosing the more vulnerable or personal aspects of their lives. Sometimes we need to listen to each other at the more superficial levels before we can trust each other with the deeper matters of the soul. When we bear with each other patiently through the surface parts of each other's stories, we discover that our sharing soon moves to another level of depth and meaning. If this is true for our conversations with each other, how much more do we need to be patient in our conversations with God? Often we are in a hurry to find out what God wants for our lives, while God is in no hurry at all!

3. *Listening well usually requires a quiet and private place.* People will seldom talk about what is deepest in their heart unless there is time and privacy. Few practices have enriched my relationships with my loved ones more than spending uninterrupted time with each of them.

   I enjoy going out with each of them separately so that we can have the space to share in depth with each other in a leisurely and relaxed way. Within these conversations God has repeatedly drawn my attention to how my love can be expressed more meaningfully for those I say I love the most.

Do you see the critical connection between listening well and discerning God's personal will? As we embark on this adventure of learning how to listen to those around us—our spouse, our siblings, our friends, our colleagues—listening can become a way of life, a habit, a spiritual practice. We discover that, as this happens, listening well opens up our relationships with each other and the whole realm of the Spirit. Our conversations with God and with others become sacred. Most importantly, we receive clues for how to bring our lives and relationships more into harmony with God's will.

---

### *Discernment Exercise*

*When did you last listen well to someone, giving them attention and showing genuine interest in what they were saying? Recall that moment. Did you look at your phone while they talked or think about what you were going to say next or interrupt the conversation with advice? Let us acknowledge that we are seldom good listeners. One of my colleagues and friends teaches that the biggest blockage to listening well is our mistaken belief that we listen well when in fact we do not.[2] You might like to ask someone who knows you well and is willing to speak the truth how they experience you as a listener in your conversations.*

*The next question is this: When did someone last listen to you with attention and genuine interest? Being listened to is surely one of the most special gifts that we can receive from another. Having someone who witnesses our life, helps us share what is most genuine within us, and treats what we say with respect is rare. Reflect on a recent experience of being listened to well and get in touch with how you felt in that conversation. We learn a great deal about what it means to listen well from others who have listened well to us.*

---

## Asking Wondering Questions

Sacred conversations involve asking *wondering questions.*

Has it ever struck you how often Jesus asked questions? It was a massive aha moment when I realized just how often in the Gospels Jesus asks questions. In my early years of following Jesus, he was introduced to me as the ultimate answer man. Certainly Jesus does answer some of the most important questions we ask. As we follow him through the Gospels, however, we see that Jesus is also the great questioner. Surveys tell us that while Jesus was asked 183 questions in the Gospels, he only directly answered three of them. However, he asked 307 questions.[3] He asked over a hundred questions for every answer he gave!

Here is an example of Jesus asking a question: Go back again to that Resurrection encounter with those two pilgrims walking along the Emmaus road. They were on their way home after the traumatic events that happened on that first Good Friday. Their dreams had been shattered when Jesus was crucified. They had pinned their hopes on him being the long-awaited Messiah who would liberate their nation. When he was killed, their hopes were killed as well. They were dejected and in despair—and then a stranger joined them. It was the risen Jesus, but they did not recognize him. He asked them a question: "What are you talking about as you walk along?" (Luke 24:17, CEB).

If you read the rest of the story, you will see that this question opened the door to an ongoing discussion between the Stranger and the two pilgrims. It led to them inviting the Stranger home with them and eventually recognizing him as the risen Jesus. This is the power of a good question.

It can open the door to the kind of conversation that enables us to discern how God may be present and active in our lives. We see this happening repeatedly in the Gospel encounters between Jesus and others around him. He has a wonderful way of drawing people into deeper reflection on their lives through the questions he asks. He is the master of knowing how to initiate sacred conversations!

There are two categories of questions that we can ask. One kind *restricts* the conversation. These questions can block further discussion, make the other person uncomfortable, put them on the spot, and/or invade their private space. They seldom communicate genuine interest, concern, and compassion. Usually they look for a yes or no answer.

The other kind *expands* the conversation. These questions invite new possibilities, enlarge the other person's arena of exploration, and help them put into words what is deepest within their heart. They communicate our desire to understand and learn more about them. They often include the words *how, what, where, when,* and *in what ways.* We could call this second category *wondering questions.* They make possible those sacred conversations that shed light on how God could be leading us. They invite thoughtfulness, facilitate reflection, and encourage discussion.

Good conversational partners know how to ask wondering questions. Besides listening well to the struggles and stirrings of our heart, they also can wonder *with* us about the meaning of what we are talking about. "How do you feel about what happened?" "What led up to you making this decision?" "Where do you see your present path taking you?" "When do you feel most alive and energized during the day?" "In what ways do you think this choice will stretch you and invite you to grow?" These kinds of questions get us to pause, reflect, and discern where God may be present and active in our inner and outer lives.

---

## Discernment Exercise

*Recall a time when you were asked a question that blocked conversation. What was the question you were asked? How did you feel when you were asked this question? In what way did this question restrict the conversation?*

*Recall a time when you were asked a question that opened up conversation. What was the question you were asked? How did you feel when you were asked this question? In what way did this question expand the conversation?*

*Reflect on the difference between these two conversational encounters. What do you learn about asking wondering questions?*

---

## Sharing What Is Most Real

Sacred conversations involve sharing what is most real.

While James encourages us "to be slow to speak and quick to listen," we do also need to speak. It has taken me time to learn this. Because I place great value on listening to others and asking those wondering questions, I sometimes hold back from sharing what is most real in my own life. One day, my daughter said to me, "Dad, you hide behind your listening!" More recently, I have been learning to be more generous in letting others glimpse my thoughts and what is happening in my life. Putting words to what is happening within us often sheds light on the next step we need to take in life.

Each of us has our own unique story to tell. From the moment of our conception, God has been actively present in every experience, encounter, and event of our lives. Every time we share aspects of our story and engage with the unique story of the other person, we have an opportunity to notice how God may be at work within us to realize God's dream for us. This can be a wonderful stepping stone in learning to live adventurously with God. It is through listening to the stories of others, asking wondering questions, *and* sharing our own story that we begin to discern God's personal will for us. This is the precious gift of sacred conversations.

Whenever we choose to speak about ourselves, we face a choice: Are we going to reveal what is most real, or are we going to hide what is most real? Think about your last few significant conversations. Were you able to express what was really going on in your heart and mind, or did you feel pressure to impress the other person and communicate a certain image of yourself? It can be helpful to become more aware of how we make conversation with those around us. Sacred conversations take place when we can speak honestly, truthfully, and simply from our heart rather than from a place of wanting to look good in front of the other person. This is the case for our conversations with each other and with God.

To move toward sharing what is most real, we need to learn to speak in the first person. This can be quite challenging initially. Imagine what it would be like for you to begin your sentences with phrases like *I feel that, I think that, I hope that, I long for, I believe that, I sense that, I wonder about, I am fearful of, I am angry about*, and so on. We would find ourselves speaking more personally, more directly, and more simply. Our conversations would shift to another level of depth and meaning. Our capacity for listening to the Spirit's movement in our heart would be fine-tuned. Discerning God's personal will would become a greater reality.

## Discernment Exercise

*You may not have ever really shared in this kind of sacred conversation. Arrange a time to meet with someone you know well to try it out.*

*One way you can prepare as you experiment, either with a close friend or in a group, is to reflect on the story of your life as if you were writing a book. Here are some wondering questions you can explore together:*

- *If you were to write the story of your life, what title would you give your book?*
- *What would the chapters of your life story be titled?*
- *What is the title of your current chapter?*
- *Where in your life are you seeking to discern God's personal will presently?*
- *What longings do you have for the chapter you are now living?*

*It may be best to prepare for this conversation by taking time beforehand to reflect on your life and make some notes. After you have shared your responses to these questions and listened to the reflections of those with you, notice how you felt and what you thought during the conversation. Did your heart burn at any time? Remember that God's Spirit leads us through those inner movements of consolation.*

## Practicing Sacred Conversations

I hope I have encouraged you to engage in more sacred conversations. Would it not be life-giving if our faith communities could become safe spaces for such conversational encounters to take place? Perhaps you could relate in this way with someone in your small faith group and with someone in your family and friendship circle. Or maybe you can engage with someone who is reading this book with you.

When we do listen well to each other, ask wondering questions of one another, and share what is most real, we position ourselves to discern God's personal will much more clearly and responsibly. May having sacred conversations with those around you become a natural way of life!

*Part Three*

# PRACTICING

# GOD'S

# WILL

*Chapter 9*

# MAKING FAITHFUL DECISIONS

*Among our loneliest moments is the time of decision.*

DALLAS WILLARD

Thus far we have been exploring how to discern God's personal will. We move now to the task of making faithful decisions. Unless we make faithful choices, all our time and effort given to discernment will be wasted. Just the other day, I came across a post on social media from a millennial seemingly disillusioned with her teenage faith. She wrote,

> As an evangelical teen, I spent an exorbitant amount of time trying to discern God's will for my life. I could've spent it learning skills of decision making, taking responsibility, learning from failures, and trying new things. Missed opportunity.[1]

Her point is well made. Our understanding of discernment must link prayer and action. Discernment without decision-making remains incomplete. Imagine a person who spends their whole life discerning, reflecting, and praying about how God may be calling them to serve yet never gets around to deciding how they will extend God's will where they live and work. They will go to their grave not having delivered their message, sung their song, or bestowed the act of love that was theirs alone to give. Hauntingly, as the post puts it, a "missed opportunity."

## What Decision Should I Make?

God has created us with amazing freedom to decide what kind of person we want to become and what we want to do. We give expression to this God-given dignity as image bearers when we face the complex decisions that come our way, consider our options, weigh our choices, and then consciously decide the way we want to go. Every decision we make matters. They shape our heart, define our character, and make up our life. As Carlos Valles has written, "To choose is to live, and as I understand and refine my ways of choosing and deciding and making up my mind, I understand better and refine more effectively my own life."[2]

Our decisions also express our desire to be faithful to God's personal will. A basic conviction of this book is that because God has both a general and personal will for our lives, we must endeavor to discern what God wants for us. I am hoping that the building blocks of discernment we have looked at so far have been helpful. Our efforts at discerning God's calling must now result in decision-making, however. Discernment needs to be lived out in our daily choices. Through the everyday decisions we make, we seek to bring our lives into harmony with what God wants for our life and for our world.

Since you are still reading this book, I assume that this is what you want to do: love, serve, and praise God in all you do. You are seeking to live a discerning life by aligning your life with God, listening to God in Scripture, paying attention to the inner movements of your heart, uncovering your unique giftedness, reflecting on your life circumstances, and engaging in sacred conversations. Now your praying needs to go something like this: *God, please help me make faithful decisions so that your Kingdom may come and your will be done on earth,* in and through me, *as it is done in heaven.*

This is not always a straightforward matter. To begin with, our decisions come in different shapes and sizes. On the one hand, consider those momentous decisions that shape your life forever.

Think of the choices that involve what and where we will study, what we will do careerwise, whether we will marry or remain single, whether we will start our own business or work for someone else, and how we will serve God within the church and out in the wider community. How do we go about making faithful decisions about these major life choices?

On the other hand are smaller decisions we need to make throughout the day. These involve how we might plan our day, how we respond to difficult emails, what we ought to give our attention to, and what we will leave for another day. While they may look small, every choice we make shapes our life for better or worse. These daily choices are often the ones we make while we are on the move. We have little time to pray over them or reflect on them for long. They bombard us, one after another, demanding an immediate response. What does faithful decision-making look like in the hurly-burly of everyday living?

Many times, these decisions, both big and small, are not obviously between good and evil. I trust that as Christ followers, we have already decided to do whatever good seems to be God's personal will. Making faithful decisions is more straightforward when we must choose between what is clearly in harmony with God's general will as revealed in Scripture and what is not. However, there are times when we need to make decisions where all the options in front of us are good. When we love God and genuinely want to discern God's personal will, making faithful decisions in these kinds of situations can be difficult. How often have you wondered, *What should I do here?* when wrestling between two or more good and positive options?

## Discernment Exercise

*Think of a recent decision you made. How did you go about making it? How was your decision-making process related to the question of God's personal will? What factors did you take into consideration in making your decision? How did you feel before and after the decision? Make some notes as you reflect on this. Becoming more aware of how you have made past decisions will help you integrate your present decision-making processes more consciously with your desire to be faithful to God's will.*

### Asking for God's Guidance

When there is no clear biblical imperative to guide us, a good starting point is to tell God that we want to be faithful and open to whatever God wants.[3] This is important. We are saying that we want to live faithfully no matter what God may want us to do. We need to be honest about this, however. It could be that we already lean toward one option more than others. Or we may have mixed feelings about doing what God may want us to do. Then we might pray something like *Lord, I know that right now I am not able to be totally open to what you might want. Please help me want to do your will with more of myself.*

The next step is to lay the situation facing us before God and specifically ask for the divine gift of guidance. We can do this with a quiet confidence that God will communicate with us *should* there be something that God wants to say to us. *Lord,* we can pray, *I want to make a faithful decision in this situation. Help me be open to whatever you may want to say. Speak to me through the people who cross my path, or through my thoughts and feelings, or through the circumstances of my life, or in my moments of silence, and especially through the Scriptures as I pray with them.*

When we have prayed like this, there occasionally may come soon afterward what we call "a clear word from the Lord." We will know immediately, with a deep assurance, what our decision must be. Possible questions or concerns that we may have had will fade away. You may have had this kind of experience.

A distinctive thought presents itself with a quiet authority, a certain clarity, a Christlike tone. You just know what you must do, and you are able to make your decision. Nevertheless, if the decision is a big one, it may still be wise to talk it over in a sacred conversation with a loved one, a trusted friend, or a counselor. Sometimes it is helpful to ask God for this word to be confirmed in one way or another.

When no clear word like this comes, however, we should simply proceed with our lives as usual, paying attention to what happens in both the inner *and* outer landscapes of our life. When we consider the different options facing us, we can weigh which one seems to lead us toward greater faith, hope, and love. Which one makes us feel genuinely alive? Which one gives us a profound sense of peace? What course of action seems to resonate more with the way of Christ? Also, which of the options leaves us with a sense of heaviness and disquiet? Remember the guideline we established in chapter 5: *The Holy Spirit always leads and guides us through spiritual consolation.* If our basic aim in life is to do God's will, it follows that whatever decision is in tune with God's purpose will bring us alive and fill us with a settled peace.

We can also reflect on what is going on in the external circumstances of our life. I recently shared in a Quaker meeting for worship. As you may know, Quakers meet in silence. Worshipers only speak if they are prompted by the Spirit. Near the end of this meeting, a woman shared her dilemma about decisions she needed to make regarding her studies in a volatile university environment. She ended by sharing with us how helpful she was finding a Quaker saying: *Proceed as the way opens for you.* I found those words helpful too. As we reflect on the outer landscape of our lives, the Spirit sometimes guides us through surprising openings in our circumstances and doors that suddenly open for us.

Whichever way God may guide us in our decision-making, let us not make an idol of needing to be right. There is always the possibility that we may read God's signals wrong. This does not mean that we should be anxious when making decisions. We can trust that God knows the desire of our heart to be faithful. As we remain open to God's future leadings, we can be sure that God will ultimately weave all our decisions into the tapestry of purpose that God has for our lives.

---

### Discernment Exercise

*Think of a situation in your life right now in which a decision needs to be made. (Preferably, experiment with a small decision.) Put the steps outlined here into practice. Share with God your desire to do whatever God wants. Lay the situation you are facing before God, and ask for the gift of guidance. Be open to God speaking to you. Pay attention to the inner movements of your heart. Reflect on the external circumstances of your life. You may find the process a bit complicated. However, I have found that the more I practice it, the more it becomes part of me. Sometimes it is possible even in those quick decisions that we need to make to use these steps. Let the steps lead you toward a decision.*

---

## When No Guidance Comes

You may be thinking: *But suppose when I ask for God's guidance there is no response. No word comes from God, there is no strong inner movement, and my circumstances remain the same. What then should I do?* This is an important question that needs our careful reflection. Here are three thoughts for us to reflect on when no clear guidance is forthcoming from God.

1. *God wants us to use our common sense as mature adult children.* A simple analogy may help. Debbie and I have two grown-up children. We knew that they would only grow into maturity as they learned to make their own choices. It would not have been wise for us to always tell them what to do. Similarly, in our relationship with our heavenly Father, there come times when God will not tell us what to do. If we are going to be God's mature children, sometimes we need

to apply common sense in ways that will help us make wise decisions.

One way of doing this is to take a sheet of paper and make a list of the advantages and disadvantages that go with each option. Write down pros and cons relating to each of the possible choices. You can then evaluate the advantages and disadvantages of each option with questions like these: *Which option brings greater glory to God and serves the greater good of those around me as well as the greater good of my own life? Which option most reflects my deepest-held convictions as a Christ follower?*

2. *Sometimes God wants us to do what we most want to do.* Jesus once asked two of his disciples, "What do you want me to do for you?" (Mark 10:36, NIV). This is a question that helps us listen to our own deepest desires, discover what we most want, and follow through on it. Obviously, we should carefully sift through our desires before we act on them. Sometimes what we may want clearly goes against God's general will. At other times, we find that our deepest desire is in harmony with God's personal calling in profound ways. Let me therefore ask you: What do you most want to do for God?

3. *God wants us to be creative.* As bearers of God's image, we are made to be creative. Jesus told a startling parable of a dutiful servant who did everything that his master told him to do (Luke 17:7-10). He showed complete obedience. Yet Jesus called him "unworthy" (NIV)! If he, then, was unworthy, who is the worthy servant? The worthy servant is the one who goes *beyond* dutiful obedience. Rather than just doing

what they are told to do, they take the initiative in serving their master creatively and freely.

What God wants from us is not mere obedience but a willingness to express our love by stepping out into a world of creative initiative. One significant way this happened for me was when I decided to begin writing to share God's good news with others. It was something I had wanted to do out of love for God almost from the beginnings of my spiritual walk. Finally, in the early 1990s, with the encouragement of a few trusted friends, I took the risk and began writing. And I haven't stopped!

I wonder what this may look like in your life.

---

### Discernment Exercise

*I wonder how these three thoughts apply to your life. Consider a decision where there seems to be no clear guidance from God. Assume that God wants you to make your decision based on using your common sense, doing what you would most want to do for God, and/or exercising your creative initiative. What is your decision? It is in moments like these, when no specific guidance comes, that our decisions reveal the true condition of our heart toward God.*

---

## Fulfilling the Purpose of Discernment

Faithful decisions give practical expression to our journey of discernment. They express our wish to be in harmony with God's dream for our lives and our world. They reveal our intention to live aligned with God daily. They ground our listening to God in Scripture within everyday particulars. They result from exploring our inner and outer landscapes. They demonstrate how we can best exercise our giftedness. They convert our sacred conversations into sacred actions. Faithful decisions fulfill the purpose of discernment.

*Chapter 10*

# BECOMING THE UNIQUE PERSON GOD WANTS US TO BE

*Be who God meant you to be and you will set the world on fire.*

CATHERINE OF SIENA

Have you ever witnessed a young child learning to say their name? It is beautiful to watch. At first, they make sounds that resemble their name but that are not quite right. Gradually their pronunciation becomes clearer. Eventually they can say their name properly. The sheer delight on their face as they do this brings joy to those around them. As my daughter said when she witnessed her little niece practicing her name for us on video, "There is something so beautiful about learning to pronounce your own name."

God has a unique name for each one of us. Reflecting on the name written on the white stone that we receive in the Kingdom (Revelation 2:17), Russian author Anthony Bloom has pointed out that this is not a nickname, a family name, or even what we call our Christian name. This is the special name by which God knows the real you and the real me. This name, which God spoke when we were first loved into existence, "defines our absolute and unrepeatable uniqueness as far as God is concerned."[1] As the prophet Isaiah put it, "Yahweh called me before I was born; from my mother's womb, he pronounced my name" (Isaiah 49:1, author's paraphrase).

Nothing is more important than learning this unique name God has for us. This involves blossoming into the person God wants us to be. Becoming who we are really is the essential aim of our life with God. Important as it is that we discern what God calls us to *do*, it is vital that we become who God created us to *be*. Some may be hesitant about this bold assertion. Surely as Christ followers our goal is to bring glory to God. Certainly! And the best way to glorify God is by maturing into our unique selves. As we fulfill the destiny God has for us, we learn the exclusive name by which God calls us. We show up in the world as God intends.

Human beings seem to be the one part of God's creation that resist this. Debbie and I have two Yorkie puppies—Lofty and Buddy. They delight in being what God has created them to be! They do not pretend to be anything other than who they are. They bring glory to God (and joy to us!) simply by being Lofty and Buddy. The same goes for the rest of creation. The flowers in the garden, the clouds in the sky, the trees in the forest, and the stones on the pathway all glorify God by being the unique flowers, clouds, trees, or stones that they were created to be. In contrast, great barriers, both inside and outside us, keep us from fulfilling our destiny as God's unique image bearers.

One of the biggest obstacles is our tendency to regard *what we do* as more important than *who we become*. Just this week I was talking with someone who walks with me on my own journey with God. I was describing for her the increasing diminishments that I was facing as I got older. Much as I would like it to be an exception to the norm, I can simply no longer do some things. She smiled as I explained these limitations, and then quietly said, "Trevor, I pray that as your 'doing' becomes more limited, your 'being' may expand." She was inviting me to learn to pronounce my own name more clearly. Even in my early seventies!

It seems fitting that we end our exploration of God's personal will by looking at this "being" dimension of our individual calling. Recall for a moment the three selves described in the first chapter: our external self, our present self, and our becoming self. They are not three separate and unrelated parts of who we are; rather, they reflect the three senses in which we continually live our daily lives. There is the *external self,* which we show to the world; the *present self,* which exists just beneath the surface of our lives and is often known only to those close to us; and the *becoming self,* who is the unique person that God's Spirit is continually weaving into being as we bring more of all three selves to the living Christ.

In this chapter, we will explore how we can more fully become the unique person God wants us to be. Our exploration has two sides. On the one hand, Christ, through his Spirit, transforms us into who God wants us to be. On the other hand, we need to cooperate with the Spirit in this transforming activity. I hope that as we engage this part of God's personal will more intentionally, we will learn to pronounce our God-given name more clearly.

---

### Discernment Exercise

*Reflect for a few moments on the relationship between what you do and who you are becoming. How would you describe it? To which dimension do you give more attention? Share with the Lord your feelings and thoughts about how being and doing are connected in your life.*

---

## Opening to the Spirit

The powerful work of the Holy Spirit in our lives is transforming us into the person God wants us to be. In his second letter to the Corinthians, Paul describes this lifelong process: "We all, who with unveiled faces contemplate the Lord's glory, are being transformed into his image with ever-increasing glory, which comes from the Lord, who is the Spirit" (2 Corinthians 3:18, NIV). Blossoming into our true selves means allowing ourselves to be transformed by the Divine Love made present in our hearts and minds by the Holy Spirit and letting God change us from the inside out.

It is so important for us to grasp this. Becoming who God intends us to be is not a self-help scheme or a self-improvement program, or about knocking ourselves into shape or "just being ourselves." Sometimes just being myself may look rather self-centered and mean! Rather, it involves opening our exterior self and our present self to the transforming activity of the Holy Spirit within us. Then the risen Christ can deliver us from all that keeps us from becoming the true self God has destined us to be. This is how the Spirit helps us blossom into the unique and unrepeatable person God wants us to be.

Paul's words above remind us that this journey of being gradually transformed by the Spirit into God's image is personal but not private. The pronoun *we* reminds us that the Holy Spirit transforms us within the environment of our friendships inside God's family. As we open ourselves to each other and engage in what I have called sacred conversations, we give the Spirit more scope to change us inwardly. Gradually, our unique capacity for reflecting the image of Christ is released. Blossoming into who God wants us to be is never a solitary operation. It happens within the community of friends Christ brings into our lives.

But we also need to say something about how we can open ourselves more fully to the Holy Spirit each day. God is not pushy. Nor does God gate-crash our lives. God always respects our freedom in our relationships with each other. With God, little happens automatically. The Holy Spirit is not going to fill us without our consent. So how do we allow the Spirit to flow more fully into our hidden depths? Paul gives us one important clue: Those who are transformed are those "who with unveiled faces contemplate the Lord's glory." We open our hearts and minds to the transforming work of the Holy Spirit as we learn how to *contemplate* the glory of God.

When it comes to contemplating the Lord with an unveiled face, I can see further than I have traveled.

However, let me share with you what I am learning. To contemplate the glory of God is not some private, cozy religious experience reserved for the "spiritually elite."

Simply put, contemplation is learning to live transparently, simply, and lovingly before God and those around us. It pays attention to what is most real within and around us. It turns our gaze away from ourselves toward our Creator, whose glory radiates through all things. It surrenders to the Divine Love streaming toward us in Christ. It looks at others with more generous, compassionate, nonjudgmental eyes. It beholds the hidden beauty in the person next to us. In the words of the great hymn writer

Charles Wesley, it allows us, in the presence of God, to be "lost in wonder, love, and praise."[2]

---

### Discernment Exercise

*Learning to live contemplatively requires much grace and takes a bit of practice. Here is a simple way to begin: Go outside one night and simply look up at the stars, the moon, the sky. Allow the heavens to "declare the glory of God" to you (Psalm 19:1, NIV). For a few moments, forget about yourself and take in the vastness of God's world. Allow yourself to feel your own smallness and finiteness. Let yourself be "lost in wonder, love, and praise." Open yourself to the Spirit of God, who is present throughout all creation. Regularly from now on, ask God to teach you how to contemplate the glory of the Lord with an unveiled face, as Paul suggests.*

---

## Cooperating with the Spirit

Our ongoing transformation into the person God wants us to be involves a division of labor. Certainly, as we have seen, it is an internal work of the Spirit, a gracious gift given to those who learn to contemplate the glory of the Lord with unveiled faces. Yet the moment we learn this, we dare not make the tragic mistake of thinking that there is nothing we must do. Faith without action is dead (James 2:26). Inner transformation requires our intentional cooperation. Learning to pronounce our own name takes effort. But what are we to do?

Here are three practices in cooperating with the Spirit that you may find helpful: rejoicing in our own uniqueness, noticing our tendency to pretend, and listening to the "sound of the genuine" within.

## Rejoicing in Our Own Uniqueness

It is rare to meet someone who genuinely rejoices in being the unique expression of God's handiwork that they are. We tend to look at those around us and wish we were more like them. They seem to be happier, freer, more successful—and the list goes on. If we could look like they do, we would be happier. If we could have what they have, we would be freer. If we could relate like they do, we would be more successful. The comparison trap ambushes us repeatedly, leaving us discontented with who we are and wishing we were someone else. We feel that we lack something vital.

I remember a time in my early thirties when I wished I resembled one of my older colleagues. He was an extrovert whose warm and humorous presence lit up the room. One memory comes back to me. We were sitting in our lounge with a visiting overseas preacher. The two were delighting in each other's company, sharing funny stories, engaging in brilliant repartee. While it was wonderful to be with them, part of me also wished that I had my colleague's ability to be as funny and smart as he was. Instead of being able to rejoice in his uniqueness, I saw him as a yardstick of what I wanted to be like as a minister.

Slowly, over the years, some biblical truths about who we are began to seep into my soul. Each of us was uniquely created in our mother's womb (Psalm 139:13-14). We are individually precious to the Good Shepherd, who searches for the one sheep that is lost (Luke 15:3-7).

Each one of us is called by name by the Shepherd who goes ahead of us (John 10:3). Verses like these, and there are many more, remind us that we are wonderfully different from those with whom we compare ourselves. We are not meant to be like them, and they are not meant to be like us. What they need, and what the world needs, is for us as unique image bearers to shape a life that has never been lived before.

Rejoicing in our own uniqueness frees us to revel in the uniqueness of everyone around us. We delight in who they are. We help them express their giftedness. We support their flourishing. We pray for their success. We celebrate their achievements. We become freer to love and to accept them for who they are. This is what those around us most need from us. They do not need us to make them a standard that we must imitate. This not only inhibits the transforming work of the Spirit in our relationships with each other but also prevents us from making our own distinctive contribution to them. Can you see why the greatest gift to our family and friends is for us to rejoice in our uniqueness?

### Noticing Our Tendency to Pretend

What we love about children is their lack of pretense. They have not learned to hide themselves yet. We can see their hearts in their faces, their words, and their actions. As we get older, we gradually discover the art of packaging ourselves. Our internal marketing manager begins to cultivate the exterior self to look more successful, self-sufficient, and virtuous than we really are. Our present self, with its fears and tears, becomes more and more hidden. The chasm between our public image and our inner reality grows bigger and wider. Pretense becomes a way of life. As depth psychologist David Benner has written, "Most adults know the occasional feeling of being a fraud—a sense of being not what they pretend to be but rather precisely what they pretend *not* to be."[3]

The consequences are sad. Pretense alienates us from both God and those around us. Every authentic encounter, divine or human, involves transparency. Living a lie with our family, our friends, our colleagues, our congregation, and our Creator alienates us from knowing the depth and richness of true relationship. Perhaps the saddest consequence is how pretense keeps us from becoming the unique person God wants us to be. Rather than knowing the freedom of being who we truly are, we become attached to this false image of ourselves. We do not learn to pronounce the true name that God has given us.

Being aware of our tendency to pretend leads us deeper into the mystery of our uniqueness. Sometimes these "pretend moments," while they may seem trivial, can be quite revealing. Recently I was doing a Zoom call with an overseas group studying one of my books. I wanted to finish the call at 7:00 p.m. my time because that was when my favorite soccer team was playing on TV. By 7:00 p.m. the group was still eagerly involved in conversation. In front of me were two used coffee cups. Wanting to end the call, I said that I needed to go to the kitchen to do my kitchen duties. I thought that would make me look rather virtuous. The call ended, and I quickly took the coffee cups to the kitchen so that I could watch the game. Full marks for pretense!

I could live with my pretense for about two hours. Straightaway after the game I emailed my host. I told him I had not been totally honest. The dirty coffee cups could have remained unwashed a bit longer. The truth was that I wanted to watch my team play soccer. Would he please tell the group members and not give up on me just yet? His immediate email response was filled with grace and humor. "Trevor—too funny about the soccer game you wanted to see! I thought the dishwashing was a bit of a flimsy excuse, but soccer—definitely a good reason to end abruptly."

The journey from pretense into authenticity takes a lifetime!

### Listening to the "Sound of the Genuine" Within

The late philosopher of religion and civil rights activist Howard Thurman guides us greatly in this task of becoming who God wants us to be. In his 1980 baccalaureate address at Spelman College, he invited the graduating students to listen to the "sound of the genuine" in their lives.[4] He reminded them that if they failed to pay attention to the sound of the genuine, they would spend all their lives "on the ends of strings that somebody else pulls." They would also never find what it was that they were really searching for. If, however, they did listen to the "sound of the genuine" and then did not follow it, it would have been better that they "had never been born." He said this sound was the one true guide they had in discovering the mystery of their own uniqueness.

How do we listen to the "sound of the genuine" within? One way we can do this is to pay attention to what makes us feel alive. What brings us to a more alive state gives us clues to who we are meant to be. Perhaps what gives you life is painting landscapes, or writing poetry, or baking cakes, or cultivating the garden, or fixing cars, or listening deeply to others, or preparing a talk, or selling a product, or negotiating business deals, or praying with others, or exploring ideas about science and faith; the list is endless. When you have paid attention to what gives you life, contrast it with the things that really drain you. Noticing this difference sharpens our ability to hear what "the genuine" sounds like in our lives.

Once we have some understanding of what enlivens us, we can give more time to those activities. We can begin to live more in tune with who we are. As we live more truly into the self that was knitted together in our mother's womb, we will not only fulfill our personal destiny but also find deeper communion with those around us.

Listening to the "sound of the genuine" within also frees us to be attentive to this sound in the lives of our loved ones, our friends, and even in the person we do not like. As Thurman once said to someone seeking his advice, "Don't ask what the world needs. Ask what makes you come alive and go do that, because what the world needs is more people who have come alive."[5]

---

### Discernment Exercise

*Spend time experimenting with each of these practices. You could begin by thanking God regularly for the gift of your life. If you find this difficult, ask God to help you rejoice in the mystery of your own uniqueness.*

*With God's help, reflect on your tendency to pretend. Consider the ways your inner marketing manager works. Share these reflections with the One who has created you and loves you without conditions.*

*Make a list of those activities that genuinely make you feel alive and those that drain you. Develop an awareness of what is life-giving for you and what is deadening. How can you give more time to what enlivens you?*

---

## Learning to Pronounce Our Own Name

My daughter was right. There is something beautiful about learning to pronounce our own name. This is God's personal will for you and me. It goes beyond merely discerning what God wants us to do. It involves becoming the unique person God wants us to be. This is what it means to be "called by name." As we regularly seek to discern God's personal will for us, we increasingly lead lives of faithfulness and purpose. We deliver our special message, we sing our special song for others, and we bestow our special act of love. This is what we were born to *be* and to do. This is how we bring glory to God.

# Afterword

Dear reader,

After you have turned the last page, I wonder how this book is landing with you. I wonder if the longing that brought you here and kept you engaged has led you to encounter God. It certainly has for me. Trevor had my attention in chapter 1:

> "God sends each person into this world with a special message to deliver, with a special song to sing for others, with a special act of love to bestow."[1] No one else can speak my message, or sing my song, or offer my act of love. These are entrusted only to me.

Can you hear the whispers of your song? Are you noticing love as it swells and spills out of your life? Is the message that God has asked you to share becoming clearer?

In 2011, I attended a Renovaré retreat in Colorado Springs and heard Trevor speak for the first time. I remember the weight and gentle conviction with which he communicated. He spoke like a man who had road tested every thought and idea shared. Perhaps you have noticed this too. When Trevor invited us to ponder God's big dream and to participate in keeping it alive, I sensed he's spent his life learning to live this way.

Trevor's practical, honest, and helpful guidance flows from his life of shared intimacy with God, and as a result, the discernment exercises at the end of each chapter are helpful! We can know and hear God's will when we have experienced the reality that "divine compassion fills the whole being of God." The debilitating pressure to know God's will isn't some capricious guessing game of feigned certainty but an invitation to become more fully ourselves in harmony with who God is and God's love for our world.

Listening to our "inner landscape" and "outer landscape" is crucial for this harmony. We bring our thoughts and feelings, our past and present, our movements toward God and our movements away from God into discerning conversations. All our experiences are part of our life with God, and they are all part of our listening life. The gifts and talents we bring, our life circumstances, and even the state of our sacred and scarred world all add their voices to our listening for God. Trevor offers us the gift of the prayer of Examen to steward these precious landscapes.

There are challenges along this sacred way of listening for God's will. Surrender is required, but a careful surrender. Trevor reminds us, "We can only truly surrender ourselves to God when we have a real life to surrender, broken and imperfect as it may be." In the past you may have found Scripture to be helpful or challenging—or both. We are reminded to keep company with Christ and let Christ, whose name we bear and whose friendship we enjoy, teach us. The ever-present Christ, Immanuel ("God with us"), will guide us through treacherous waters when we ask.

We don't stop with prayerful pondering but are invited to participate, to act upon what we have discerned with the Spirit's help. For me, this is where the ride gets wild. Knowing in our bones that God knows the real you, the real me, loves us with an ever-lasting love, and invites us to participate in the big dream is mind-blowing, abundant-life stuff. We follow the consolations the Spirit has laid out for us like little breadcrumbs drawing us to dream, create, and contribute to the good God is doing.

However, *doing* isn't the end of things. This isn't a linear jour-ney; it's a circular one leading us back to *who* we are in Christ. As Trevor and his daughter put it, we "[learn] to pronounce our own name." We become more fully ourselves with what Howard Thurman called "the sound of the genuine" ringing through all parts of our lives.[2]

I'll leave you with Trevor's words of encouragement from chapter 1:

> *You have been desired into existence by a Great Love. You are meant to be here. You are known by name. You have been chosen. You have been called by name. Your life has a unique, God-given meaning. Your unrepeatable life matters.*

*Lacy Finn Borgo*
author and spiritual director

# Outline for Groups Using This Book

My hope is that this book will become a helpful resource for small groups. This group journey does not need to be complicated. You will need a leader to facilitate the conversation, ensure that each person has an opportunity to share their thoughts and feelings, and see to it that the group begins and ends at the advertised times. Below you will find some tips for the group leader for facilitating and structuring the group time. The ideal group size is between six and twelve people. Timewise, anything between ninety minutes and two hours (depending on the group's size) works well. Always remember that our search for God's will happens best within the context of friendship and community.

## Tips for the Group Leader

- Pray for each person in your group by name and ask that they will be drawn into a deeper friendship with God.

- Encourage participants to read the chapter you will be discussing before they come to the meeting. Invite them to listen to what God may be saying to them.

- Encourage each person to say something during the time together. Sometimes a simple wondering question may be helpful, such as "How did you find this chapter?" or "What stood out to you?"

- Enhance the quality of the group conversation by reminding group members not to interrupt, argue with, or try to correct each other.

- Pay particular attention to how each person has interacted with the discernment exercises.

- Remind the group of the importance of confidentiality. What is shared in the group stays in the group.

## Possible Group Structure

- As an icebreaker, share a joy or a struggle from the past week.

- Have a brief time of prayer.

- Discuss what you found most helpful in this chapter and what you struggled with the most.

- Share your experience of engaging with the discernment exercises in the chapter.

- Pray for one another's prayer requests, either silently or aloud, before concluding your time together for the week.

# The Discipline of
# Daily Scripture Reading

Frequently I meet people who, while they may be tired of religion, yearn for a firsthand relationship with God that will empower their lives with a fresh sense of vision. They are hungry for a living spirituality. Reflecting upon my conversations with these seekers after God, I've noticed a remarkable similarity in the yearning expressed. They ask questions like "How do I come to know God?" and "How can I deepen my friendship with God?" and "How do I find out God's will for my life?" Usually I respond with one sentence: *Keep company with Jesus in the Gospels.*

How do we go about doing this? Allow me to be practical and straightforward in my response. Each day read a short Gospel passage, one that is small enough to be digested without hurry. As you read, keep company with Jesus. Try to understand his feelings about God, notice the way he relates to people, listen to the message he brings, meditate on his teachings, and watch what he does. Consider always what meaning all this would hold for you if you were to live your life as Jesus would if he were in your place.

Inside this list you will find readings from one of the Gospels or the book of Acts for each day of the year. Whereas the chapter divisions are usually too long to digest in one sitting, the following units are deliberately short, and most are devoted to single topics. Following the outlined plan, you will be able to read through these five books in exactly one year.

I offer this plan of daily Bible readings to you with both confidence and hope. I include it with confidence because, as I have followed it myself, it has changed my life. I include it with hope because I am expectant that, through your meditations on these passages, God can change your life too.

| Day | Reading | | Day | Reading | | Day | Reading | |
|-----|---------|---|-----|---------|---|-----|---------|---|
| *Matthew* | | | 21 | 9:18-34 | ☐ | 42 | 16:13-23 | ☐ |
| 1 | 1:1-17 | ☐ | 22 | 9:35-10:15 | ☐ | 43 | 16:24-17:8 | |
| 2 | 1:18-25 | ☐ | 23 | 10:16-23 | ☐ | 44 | 17:9-21 | ☐ |
| 3 | 2:1-12 | ☐ | 24 | 10:24-33 | ☐ | 45 | 17:22-27 | |
| 4 | 2:13-23 | ☐ | 25 | 10:34-42 | ☐ | 46 | 18:1-14 | ☐ |
| 5 | 3:1-17 | | 26 | 11:1-19 | ☐ | 47 | 18:15-22 | |
| 6 | 4:1-11 | ☐ | 27 | 11:20-30 | ☐ | 48 | 18:23-35 | ☐ |
| 7 | 4:12-25 | | 28 | 12:1-14 | ☐ | 49 | 19:1-12 | |
| 8 | 5:1-12 | ☐ | 29 | 12:15-32 | | 50 | 19:13-30 | ☐ |
| 9 | 5:13-20 | | 30 | 12:33-42 | ☐ | 51 | 20:1-16 | |
| 10 | 5:21-32 | ☐ | 31 | 12:43-50 | ☐ | 52 | 20:17-28 | ☐ |
| 11 | 5:33-48 | | 32 | 13:1-17 | ☐ | 53 | 20:29-21:11 | |
| 12 | 6:1-15 | ☐ | 33 | 13:18-30 | | 54 | 21:12-22 | ☐ |
| 13 | 6:16-24 | | 34 | 13:31-43 | ☐ | 55 | 21:23-32 | |
| 14 | 6:25-34 | ☐ | 35 | 13:44-58 | | 56 | 21:33-46 | ☐ |
| 15 | 7:1-14 | | 36 | 14:1-12 | ☐ | 57 | 22:1-14 | |
| 16 | 7:15-29 | ☐ | 37 | 14:13-21 | | 58 | 22:15-33 | ☐ |
| 17 | 8:1-13 | | 38 | 14:22-36 | ☐ | 59 | 22:34-46 | |
| 18 | 8:14-27 | ☐ | 39 | 15:1-20 | | 60 | 23:1-12 | ☐ |
| 19 | 8:28-9:8 | | 40 | 15:21-31 | ☐ | 61 | 23:13-26 | |
| 20 | 9:9-17 | ☐ | 41 | 15:32-16:12 | | 62 | 23:27-39 | ☐ |

| Day | Reading | |
|-----|---------|---|
| 63 | 24:1-14 | ☐ |
| 64 | 24:15-31 | ☐ |
| 65 | 24:32-51 | ☐ |
| 66 | 25:1-13 | ☐ |
| 67 | 25:14-30 | ☐ |
| 68 | 25:31-46 | ☐ |
| 69 | 26:1-16 | ☐ |
| 70 | 26:17-29 | ☐ |
| 71 | 26:30-46 | ☐ |
| 72 | 26:47-56 | ☐ |
| 73 | 26:57-75 | ☐ |
| 74 | 27:1-10 | ☐ |
| 75 | 27:11-26 | ☐ |
| 76 | 27:27-44 | ☐ |
| 77 | 27:45-54 | ☐ |
| 78 | 27:55-66 | ☐ |
| 79 | 28:1-10 | ☐ |
| 80 | 28:11-20 | ☐ |
| **Mark** | | |
| 81 | 1:1-13 | ☐ |
| 82 | 1:14-28 | ☐ |
| 83 | 1:29-45 | ☐ |
| 84 | 2:1-12 | ☐ |
| 85 | 2:13-22 | ☐ |
| 86 | 2:23–3:6 | ☐ |
| 87 | 3:7-19 | ☐ |
| 88 | 3:20-35 | ☐ |
| 89 | 4:1-20 | ☐ |

| Day | Reading | |
|-----|---------|---|
| 90 | 4:21-32 | ☐ |
| 91 | 4:33-41 | ☐ |
| 92 | 5:1-20 | ☐ |
| 93 | 5:21-34 | ☐ |
| 94 | 5:35-43 | ☐ |
| 95 | 6:1-13 | ☐ |
| 96 | 6:14-29 | ☐ |
| 97 | 6:30-44 | ☐ |
| 98 | 6:45-56 | ☐ |
| 99 | 7:1-13 | ☐ |
| 100 | 7:14-30 | ☐ |
| 101 | 7:31-37 | ☐ |
| 102 | 8:1-10 | ☐ |
| 103 | 8:11-21 | ☐ |
| 104 | 8:22-30 | ☐ |
| 105 | 8:31–9:1 | ☐ |
| 106 | 9:2-13 | ☐ |
| 107 | 9:14-32 | ☐ |
| 108 | 9:33-50 | ☐ |
| 109 | 10:1-12 | ☐ |
| 110 | 10:13-22 | ☐ |
| 111 | 10:23-31 | ☐ |
| 112 | 10:32-45 | ☐ |
| 113 | 10:46-52 | ☐ |
| 114 | 11:1-11 | ☐ |
| 115 | 11:12-26* | ☐ |
| 116 | 11:27-33 | ☐ |
| 117 | 12:1-11 | ☐ |

| Day | Reading | |
|-----|---------|---|
| 118 | 12:12-17 | ☐ |
| 119 | 12:18-27 | ☐ |
| 120 | 12:28-34 | ☐ |
| 121 | 12:35-44 | ☐ |
| 122 | 13:1-13 | ☐ |
| 123 | 13:14-27 | ☐ |
| 124 | 13:28-37 | ☐ |
| 125 | 14:1-9 | ☐ |
| 126 | 14:10-21 | ☐ |
| 127 | 14:22-31 | ☐ |
| 128 | 14:32-42 | ☐ |
| 129 | 14:43-52 | ☐ |
| 130 | 14:53-65 | ☐ |
| 131 | 14:66-72 | ☐ |
| 132 | 15:1-15 | ☐ |
| 133 | 15:16-32 | ☐ |
| 134 | 15:33-41 | ☐ |
| 135 | 15:42-47 | ☐ |
| 136 | 16:1-8 | ☐ |
| 137 | 16:9-20 | ☐ |
| **Luke** | | |
| 138 | 1:1-17 | ☐ |
| 139 | 1:18-38 | ☐ |
| 140 | 1:39-56 | ☐ |
| 141 | 1:57-66 | ☐ |
| 142 | 1:67-80 | ☐ |
| 143 | 2:1-14 | ☐ |
| 144 | 2:15-32 | ☐ |

* The careful reader will note that some Bible translations omit Mark 11:26. The KJV version of this verse reads, "But if ye do not forgive, neither will your Father which is in heaven forgive your trespasses." Those translators who omit this verse argue that it was added by later scribes to Mark's Gospel. While a full discussion of this issue is well beyond this note, it is worth noting that all translators of the Gospels certainly agree that Jesus said these words. They are recorded for us in Matthew 6:15 in all Bible translations.

| Day | Reading |
|-----|---------|
| 145 | 2:33-40 |
| 146 | 2:41-52 |
| 147 | 3:1-9 |
| 148 | 3:10-22 |
| 149 | 3:23-38 |
| 150 | 4:1-15 |
| 151 | 4:16-30 |
| 152 | 4:31-44 |
| 153 | 5:1-16 |
| 154 | 5:17-26 |
| 155 | 5:27-39 |
| 156 | 6:1-11 |
| 157 | 6:12-26 |
| 158 | 6:27-38 |
| 159 | 6:39-49 |
| 160 | 7:1-10 |
| 161 | 7:11-23 |
| 162 | 7:24-35 |
| 163 | 7:36-50 |
| 164 | 8:1-15 |
| 165 | 8:16-25 |
| 166 | 8:26-39 |
| 167 | 8:40-56 |
| 168 | 9:1-9 |
| 169 | 9:10-17 |
| 170 | 9:18-27 |
| 171 | 9:28-36 |
| 172 | 9:37-50 |
| 173 | 9:51-62 |
| 174 | 10:1-16 |
| 175 | 10:17-24 |
| 176 | 10:25-37 |

| Day | Reading |
|-----|---------|
| 177 | 10:38–11:4 |
| 178 | 11:5-13 |
| 179 | 11:14-28 |
| 180 | 11:29-36 |
| 181 | 11:37-52 |
| 182 | 11:53–12:12 |
| 183 | 12:13-21 |
| 184 | 12:22-34 |
| 185 | 12:35-48 |
| 186 | 12:49-59 |
| 187 | 13:1-9 |
| 188 | 13:10-21 |
| 189 | 13:22-30 |
| 190 | 13:31–14:6 |
| 191 | 14:7-14 |
| 192 | 14:15-24 |
| 193 | 14:25-35 |
| 194 | 15:1-10 |
| 195 | 15:11-32 |
| 196 | 16:1-9 |
| 197 | 16:10-18 |
| 198 | 16:19-31 |
| 199 | 17:1-10 |
| 200 | 17:11-21 |
| 201 | 17:22-37 |
| 202 | 18:1-17 |
| 203 | 18:18-30 |
| 204 | 18:31-43 |
| 205 | 19:1-10 |
| 206 | 19:11-27 |
| 207 | 19:28-40 |
| 208 | 19:41–20:8 |

| Day | Reading |
|-----|---------|
| 209 | 20:9-18 |
| 210 | 20:19-26 |
| 211 | 20:27–21:4 |
| 212 | 21:5-19 |
| 213 | 21:20-28 |
| 214 | 21:29-38 |
| 215 | 22:1-13 |
| 216 | 22:14-27 |
| 217 | 22:28-38 |
| 218 | 22:39-46 |
| 219 | 22:47-62 |
| 220 | 22:63–23:5 |
| 221 | 23:6-25 |
| 222 | 23:26-38 |
| 223 | 23:39-49 |
| 224 | 23:50–24:12 |
| 225 | 24:13-27 |
| 226 | 24:28-35 |
| 227 | 24:36-53 |
| **John** | |
| 228 | 1:1-18 |
| 229 | 1:19-28 |
| 230 | 1:29-42 |
| 231 | 1:43-51 |
| 232 | 2:1-11 |
| 233 | 2:12-25 |
| 234 | 3:1-15 |
| 235 | 3:16-21 |
| 236 | 3:22-36 |
| 237 | 4:1-15 |
| 238 | 4:16-30 |
| 239 | 4:31-42 |

| Day | Reading | |
|-----|---------|---|
| 240 | 4:43-54 | ☐ |
| 241 | 5:1-18 | ☐ |
| 242 | 5:19-29 | ☐ |
| 243 | 5:30-47 | ☐ |
| 244 | 6:1-14 | ☐ |
| 245 | 6:15-24 | ☐ |
| 246 | 6:25-34 | ☐ |
| 247 | 6:35-51 | ☐ |
| 248 | 6:52-65 | ☐ |
| 249 | 6:66–7:9 | ☐ |
| 250 | 7:10-24 | ☐ |
| 251 | 7:25-36 | ☐ |
| 252 | 7:37-53 | ☐ |
| 253 | 8:1-11 | ☐ |
| 254 | 8:12-30 | ☐ |
| 255 | 8:31-47 | ☐ |
| 256 | 8:48-59 | ☐ |
| 257 | 9:1-12 | ☐ |
| 258 | 9:13-23 | ☐ |
| 259 | 9:24-41 | ☐ |
| 260 | 10:1-18 | ☐ |
| 261 | 10:19-30 | ☐ |
| 262 | 10:31-42 | ☐ |
| 263 | 11:1-16 | ☐ |
| 264 | 11:17-37 | ☐ |
| 265 | 11:38-54 | ☐ |
| 266 | 11:55–12:8 | ☐ |
| 267 | 12:9-19 | ☐ |
| 268 | 12:20-36 | ☐ |
| 269 | 12:37-50 | ☐ |
| 270 | 13:1-11 | ☐ |
| 271 | 13:12-20 | ☐ |

| Day | Reading | |
|-----|---------|---|
| 272 | 13:21-30 | ☐ |
| 273 | 13:31-38 | ☐ |
| 274 | 14:1-14 | ☐ |
| 275 | 14:15-24 | ☐ |
| 276 | 14:25-31 | ☐ |
| 277 | 15:1-11 | ☐ |
| 278 | 15:12-27 | ☐ |
| 279 | 16:1-15 | ☐ |
| 280 | 16:16-28 | ☐ |
| 281 | 16:29–17:5 | ☐ |
| 282 | 17:6-19 | ☐ |
| 283 | 17:20-26 | ☐ |
| 284 | 18:1-11 | ☐ |
| 285 | 18:12-18 | ☐ |
| 286 | 18:19-27 | ☐ |
| 287 | 18:28-40 | ☐ |
| 288 | 19:1-11 | ☐ |
| 289 | 19:12-22 | ☐ |
| 290 | 19:23-30 | ☐ |
| 291 | 19:31-42 | ☐ |
| 292 | 20:1-10 | ☐ |
| 293 | 20:11-18 | ☐ |
| 294 | 20:19-25 | ☐ |
| 295 | 20:26-31 | ☐ |
| 296 | 21:1-14 | ☐ |
| 297 | 21:15-25 | ☐ |
| **Acts** | | |
| 298 | 1:1-14 | ☐ |
| 299 | 1:15-26 | ☐ |
| 300 | 2:1-13 | ☐ |
| 301 | 2:14-36 | ☐ |
| 302 | 2:37-47 | ☐ |

| Day | Reading | |
|-----|---------|---|
| 303 | 3:1-10 | ☐ |
| 304 | 3:11-26 | ☐ |
| 305 | 4:1-12 | ☐ |
| 306 | 4:13-22 | ☐ |
| 307 | 4:23-31 | ☐ |
| 308 | 4:32–5:11 | ☐ |
| 309 | 5:12-21a | ☐ |
| 310 | 5:21b-32 | ☐ |
| 311 | 5:33-42 | ☐ |
| 312 | 6:1-15 | ☐ |
| 313 | 7:1-16 | ☐ |
| 314 | 7:17-34 | ☐ |
| 315 | 7:35-53 | ☐ |
| 316 | 7:54–8:3 | ☐ |
| 317 | 8:4-24 | ☐ |
| 318 | 8:25-40 | ☐ |
| 319 | 9:1-22 | ☐ |
| 320 | 9:23-43 | ☐ |
| 321 | 10:1-16 | ☐ |
| 322 | 10:17-33 | ☐ |
| 323 | 10:34-48 | ☐ |
| 324 | 11:1-18 | ☐ |
| 325 | 11:19-30 | ☐ |
| 326 | 12:1-11 | ☐ |
| 327 | 12:12-25 | ☐ |
| 328 | 13:1-12 | ☐ |
| 329 | 13:13-25 | ☐ |
| 330 | 13:26-41 | ☐ |
| 331 | 13:42-52 | ☐ |
| 332 | 14:1-18 | ☐ |
| 333 | 14:19-28 | ☐ |
| 334 | 15:1-21 | ☐ |

| Day | Reading |  |
|-----|---------|--|
| 335 | 15:22-35 | ☐ |
| 336 | 15:36–16:10 | ☐ |
| 337 | 16:11-24 | ☐ |
| 338 | 16:25-40 | ☐ |
| 339 | 17:1-15 | ☐ |
| 340 | 17:16-34 | ☐ |
| 341 | 18:1-17 | ☐ |
| 342 | 18:18-28 | ☐ |
| 343 | 19:1-20 | ☐ |
| 344 | 19:21-41 | ☐ |
| 345 | 20:1-16 | ☐ |

| Day | Reading |  |
|-----|---------|--|
| 346 | 20:17-38 | ☐ |
| 347 | 21:1-14 | ☐ |
| 348 | 21:15-26 | ☐ |
| 349 | 21:27-39 | ☐ |
| 350 | 21:40–22:21 | ☐ |
| 351 | 22:22-30 | ☐ |
| 352 | 23:1-15 | ☐ |
| 353 | 23:16-35 | ☐ |
| 354 | 24:1-21 | ☐ |
| 355 | 24:22–25:12 | ☐ |
| 356 | 25:13-22 | ☐ |

| Day | Reading |  |
|-----|---------|--|
| 357 | 25:23–26:11 | ☐ |
| 358 | 26:12-23 | ☐ |
| 359 | 26:24-32 | ☐ |
| 360 | 27:1-12 | ☐ |
| 361 | 27:13-32 | ☐ |
| 362 | 27:33-44 | ☐ |
| 363 | 28:1-16 | ☐ |
| 364 | 28:17-22 | ☐ |
| 365 | 28:23-31 | ☐ |

## Divine Reading

Divine reading, also known as *lectio divina*, is an age-old method of praying with the Scriptures. As you read the suggested passages each day, perhaps you may like to use this method in your reading and praying. It follows five simple steps: *place, prepare, passage, ponder,* and *pray.* These steps (what I call the five Ps) are explained in more detail on pages 51–52 of this book.

# Acknowledgments

This publication distills a lifetime of learning how to discern God's will for our lives. For some time now I have wanted to write about this theme in an accessible, helpful, and encouraging way. This book represents this hope.

So many people have helped me on this ongoing journey, and it is not possible to name them all. You know who you are, and I am grateful to you. There are, however, a few people who have accompanied me in the writing of this book, and I acknowledge you with much gratitude and appreciation.

Thank you to all those at NavPress for your encouragement and colleagueship in this venture—David Zimmerman, for opening the NavPress door to my writing efforts; Elizabeth Schroll, for your creative developmental editing; Danielle, for your careful copyediting; Ron C. Kaufmann and Laura Cruise, for your creativity in design; Deborah Gonzalez, for carefully overseeing this book project from its beginning; Robin Bermel, for your marketing enthusiasm. This partnership in the ministry of books is a grace-gift.

Thank you to colleagues and friends in the different contexts in which I often work, both in South Africa and in the USA—at

Northfield Methodist Church in Benoni, South Africa; the Jesuit Institute South Africa; the Institute for Creative Conversation; the Renovaré Institute for Christian Spiritual Formation; the Conversatio website—and for the many informal conversations we have shared about discernment and other matters of the heart.

Thank you to those who have allowed me to witness their discerning journeys with God. Listening to your unique stories has taught me much about the hidden ways of the Spirit in our lives. Much of what I have written here I have learned from each of you.

Thank you to Carolyn Arends, friend and colleague in ministry, for taking the time to read and to offer a foreword. It means a great deal. Thank you also to Lacy Borgo, for your willingness to do an afterword. It has been so good to work together in helping others listen discerningly.

I would also like to thank Deborah Owen, who read the completed galleys and helped me make small, last-minute changes.

Most importantly, thank you to my immediate family—to my children, Joni and Mark, and their marriage partners, James and Marike, for your thoughtful interest in my daily work. And to you, Debbie; how do I say thank you for your loving companionship and supportive care as we journeyed together through this challenging season in our life together? Watching Netflix with you at the end of the day is the best reward and therapy ever!

*Trevor Hudson*
Benoni, South Africa
February 2024

# Selected Bibliography

I have learned so much about discernment from the writings of other Christ followers. Here are six books that have helped me in the writing of this book.

Ackermann, Denise M. *Surprised by the Man on the Borrowed Donkey: Ordinary Blessings.* Cape Town, SA: Lux Verbi, 2014.

Barry, William A. *Paying Attention to God: Discernment in Prayer.* Notre Dame, IN: Ave Maria Press, 1990.

Gibbard, Mark. *Jesus, Liberation and Love: Meditative Reflections on Our Believing and Praying, Maturity and Service.* Oxford: A. R. Mowbray, 1982.

———. *Love and Life's Journey: Venture in Prayer.* Oxford: A. R. Mowbray, 1987.

Nouwen, Henri J. M., with Michael J. Christensen and Rebecca J. Laird. *Discernment: Reading the Signs of Daily Life.* New York: HarperOne, 2013.

Willard, Dallas. *In Search of Guidance: Developing a Conversational Relationship with God.* San Francisco: HarperSanFrancisco, 1993.

# Notes

**FOREWORD**

1. Adapted from "You Probably Won't Be Sent to Egypt . . ." by Carolyn Arends, first published in *Christianity Today*, July 16, 2013, https://www .christianitytoday.com/ct/2013/june/consolation-prize.html.

**CHAPTER 1 | ANNOUNCING GOOD NEWS**

1. I first came across these words in Francis Dewar, *Invitations: God's Calling for Everyone—Stories and Quotations to Illuminate a Journey* (London: SPCK, 1996), 9.
2. Viktor E. Frankl, *Man's Search for Meaning*, rev. ed. (New York: Washington Square Press, 1985), 97.
3. I first came across this story in Mark Gibbard, *Love and Life's Journey: Venture in Prayer* (Oxford: A. R. Mowbray, 1987), 19.
4. I am grateful to the work of Mark Gibbard, SSJE, whose writings have helped so much with my thinking in this area. (See the bibliography for two of his books.)
5. *Something Beautiful for God*, interview of Mother Teresa by Malcolm Muggeridge, directed by Peter Chafer (United Kingdom: BBC Television, 1969).

**CHAPTER 2 | UNDERSTANDING DISCERNMENT**

1. See biblical verses like Psalm 138:8; Isaiah 43:1; 45:3; Jeremiah 1:5; and Ephesians 1:11; 2:10.
2. Quoted by Klaus Bockmuehl, *Listening to the God Who Speaks: Reflections on God's Guidance from Scripture and the Lives of God's People* (Colorado Springs: Helmers and Howard, 1990), 13.

3. Charles Wesley, "O for a Thousand Tongues to Sing," 1739. Public domain.

4. Mother Teresa, *A Simple Path*, comp. Lucinda Vardey (New York: Ballantine Books, 1995), 7.

5. Donald Coggan, *Preaching: The Sacrament of the Word* (New York: Crossroad, 1988), 31–32, emphasis added.

6. As quoted in Ronald J. Sider, *Genuine Christianity: Essentials for Living Your Faith* (Grand Rapids: Zondervan, 1996), 172.

## CHAPTER 4 | LISTENING TO GOD IN SCRIPTURE

1. Jonathan Sacks, "The Spirituality of Listening," Covenant and Conversation, The Rabbi Sacks Legacy, 2016, https://rabbisacks .org/covenant-conversation/eikev/the-spirituality-of-listening.

2. Scot McKnight, *The Blue Parakeet: Rethinking How You Read the Bible* (Grand Rapids: Zondervan, 2008), 87.

3. Arthur Michael Ramsey, *God, Christ and the World: A Study in Contemporary Theology* (Eugene, OR: Wipf and Stock, 2012), 37.

## CHAPTER 5 | ATTENDING TO THE MOVEMENTS OF OUR HEART

1. For more on the Spiritual Exercises, see David L. Fleming, *Draw Me into Your Friendship: A Literal Translation and a Contemporary Reading of the Spiritual Exercises* (St. Louis: Institute of Jesuit Resources, 1996).

## CHAPTER 6 | UNCOVERING AND EXERCISING OUR GIFTS

1. Gloria Gaither and William J. Gaither, "Something Beautiful," Hanna Street Music (BMI), 1971.

## CHAPTER 7 | REFLECTING ON OUR CIRCUMSTANCES

1. Frederick Buechner, *Wishful Thinking: The Seeker's ABC*, rev. ed. (San Francisco: HarperCollins, 1993), 119.

## CHAPTER 8 | ENGAGING IN SACRED CONVERSATIONS

1. If you would like more information on how your small group or faith community can grow in the art of having "sacred conversations," contact the Institute for Creative Conversation at i4ccinfo@gmail.com. They have developed a seven-week video course aimed at cultivating sacred conversations. On each of these videos I offer a short presentation together with a group process that can be used to help participants discover how to have better conversations in their different life contexts.

2. I am in debt to my colleague Lacy Borgo for this insight.

3. See, for example, Martin B. Copenhaver, *Jesus Is the Question: The 307 Questions Jesus Asked and the 3 He Answered* (Nashville: Abingdon Press, 2014).

## CHAPTER 9 | MAKING FAITHFUL DECISIONS

1. Cindy Wang Brandt (@cindywangbrandt), Twitter, September 4, 2020, 5:59 p.m., https://x.com/cindywangbrandt/status/1302033502158823424.
2. Carlos G. Valles, *The Art of Choosing: Working through Daily Decisions and Discerning Our Path in Life* (New York: Image Books, 1989), viii.
3. I have learned much about making decisions from the Spiritual Exercises of Ignatius.

## CHAPTER 10 | BECOMING THE UNIQUE PERSON GOD WANTS US TO BE

1. Anthony Bloom, *School for Prayer* (London: Darton, Longman and Todd, 1970), quoted by Francis Dewar in *Invitations: God's Calling for Everyone—Stories and Quotations to Illuminate a Journey* (London: SPCK, 1996), 89.
2. Charles Wesley, "Love Divine, All Loves Excelling," 1747. Public domain.
3. David G. Benner, *The Gift of Being Yourself: The Sacred Call to Self-Discovery* (Downers Grove, IL: InterVarsity Press, 2004), 15.
4. Howard Thurman, "The Sound of the Genuine," baccalaureate ceremony, Spelman College, May 4, 1980, The Howard Thurmal Digital Archive, https://thurman.pitts.emory.edu/items/show/838.
5. Quoted in Lerita Coleman Brown, *What Makes You Come Alive: A Spiritual Walk with Howard Thurman* (Minneapolis: Broadleaf Books, 2023), 1, 7.

## AFTERWORD

1. Trevor first came across these words in Francis Dewar, *Invitations: God's Calling for Everyone—Stories and Quotations to Illuminate a Journey* (London: SPCK, 1996), 9.
2. Howard Thurman, "The Sound of the Genuine in You" (baccalaureate ceremony at Spelman College), May 4, 1980, https://thurman.pitts.emory .edu/items/show/838.

**NavPress is the book-publishing arm of The Navigators.**

Since 1933, The Navigators has helped people around the world bring hope and purpose to others in college campuses, local churches, workplaces, neighborhoods, and hard-to-reach places all over the world, face-to-face and person-by-person in an approach we call Life-to-Life® discipleship. We have committed together to know Christ, make Him known, and help others do the same.®

Would you like to join this adventure of discipleship and disciplemaking?

- Take a Digital Discipleship Journey at **navigators.org/disciplemaking**.
- Get more discipleship and disciplemaking content at **thedisciplemaker.org**.
- Find your next book, Bible, or discipleship resource at **navpress.com**.

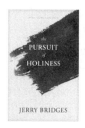    

 @NavPressPublishing

 @NavPress

 @navpressbooks

CP1790

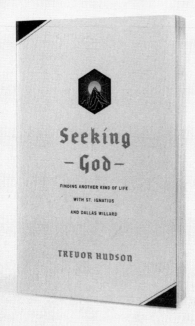